Filosofy I: Science, Ν
All Things in Betwee

For my father, God, and England.

The following is a series of essays based upon free-form journal writings composed over the summer of 2023.

Cover art by Ege Kizilarslan.

Contents

On Philosophy: An Overture

Free-Form Thoughts, handwritten in London and the Cotswolds, Summer of 2023

Philosophy can be physical. That's why builders don't need it and warriors embrace it.

One's dependence lends credibility to the other's independence.

Filosofy is like a Stairmaster. It prepares for elevation, *from peak to peak*.

Sitting in the bed of a loved one. *The being of the being comes into the constancy of its shining.*[1]

My philosophy has no intentions. It is so plain it obscures.

'Fuck off it isn't that deep.'

You can't know what I know but you can know what I like.

What words can express my love of the Cotswolds?

A true journalist creates news about himself – both subject and object.

High birthrates coexist with high satisfaction with life.

Be wary of love shown between unconditional attachments.

Stare directly into their eyes to see their real soul. All you see is black, black is the soul. Eyes can choose to or not to illuminate.

---

[1] Heidegger

The destroyer of reality. The Game-Ender. The bridge to transcendence; the touch of God?

A person of love is also a great destroyer.

Are we thinking the same thoughts?

Remain steady and unwavering.

Handwritten on Muji 64 Page, Semi-Bleached.

My philosophy is not intended to depict the world, but accompany it's movements.[2] I offer here a defence of the classical Greek understanding of the world, and of the Anglo-Saxon approximations which emerged from the Neoclassical movement, including ideas which can be considered pseudoscientific and esoteric. I do so against their lack of substantiation, against their lack of epistemic grounding, and for their utility which stands against our present reason. I do so in faith that one day they may be again justified, because for all of their irrationality, these systems and ideas, as if by magic, happen to work. Because there are things we do not yet understand, but can acquiesce to and reap benefit from until the day comes that we do.

We learned that disease was not transmitted by foul smell, so we stopped using the medieval gas mask which filtered air through good-smelling herbs. When we abandoned this incorrect assumption, and gave up using these masks, disease spread more quickly, and later we learned that our solution hundreds of years prior had worked – but not for the reasons we thought it did. Later, we realized that disease was spread by germs, so we started using filtered masks again while treating sick patients. Still later, we learned that good smelling herbs had antiseptic properties, and through science we re-justified what had initially been superstitious intuition.

We have a tendency to throw away effective measures because we fail to understand them, or because the conclusions that led us to our actions were debunked. Yet, these heuristics still work. Pseudoscience doesn't have to necessarily be true – just not wrong.

Pseudoscience, or science which lacks universal verifiability, can still be very useful as a heuristic to guide us in our lives. It can be a good rule of thumb. While pseudoscience is not applicable in all cases, the lack of universality allows for an artistic, and interpretivist approach in their application. One can use them to bend the rules of epistemology, and derive true conclusions from invisible sources, puzzling many and creating the illusion of magic. In this epistemic half-world, this front line between reason and irrationality, the stupidity of rationality and the brilliance of

---

[2] Julius Evola

madness, in this very vortex is the higher synthetic truth which can only emerge as a product of the unity of chaos and order, light and dark, it is the magic of the past, and the science of the future.

Classical philosophy and the pseudoscience derived from it was at once, before us, and after us. The uphill fight is to keep it with us, here and now, to make it the 'Filosofy' which rests, which perseveres, in the time and space between.

A new *raison d'etat,* a reason for its existence is required to justify it in the time being, until our present understanding comes into constancy with these truths that had been known, intuited, and felt. Until that happens, it is better that we stick with them rather than let them be lost. We do not know why the old ways worked, but until we do, it is imperative that we not lose the truths we have, and let all that has been built collapse. Those who beckon anarchy are captivated by a naïve illusion – they reach for the beautiful rose but grab onto a branch of thorns of suffering and contemplation.

This book is intended to serve as a temporary glue, a bulwark which holds together old conventions against the washing tide which deconstructs and washes away all that is not tied down, until we come full circle in our understanding of things.

Philosophy is inherently deconstructive, it is a force which tears down and degenerates through present reason and logic, neglecting the now lost *posteriori* context which had called ideas forth in the first place, approximating things to the lowest common denominator and reorganizing in the abstract. In doing so, ancient forms are lost, simply because we cannot any longer see the justifying impulse which called them into being. I write with faith in the old ways, the classical forms and the reason, which we no longer see, that presupposed those things once spoken into existence.

We no longer see the reason for ancient teachings, ideas, and codes of conduct – because we no longer see the reasons why they came about in the first place. Yet now, I believe we are beginning to see the inklings of those reasons emerging before us once again. We must keep them, retain them, because they will become relevant again.

We have a tendency to tear things down because we no longer see their purpose, relevance or rationale. Be they the British monarchy and aristocracy, the relevance of zodiac signs, sexual monogamy, Christian values, or the science of the four humours – in all cases a lack of understanding of why we had them to begin with precipitates their abandonment. As we deconstruct these things, we quickly move to uphold new ideals and aspirations which structure our social thought and action, looking to new idols such as Princess Diana, scientific positivism, and the Jenner/ Kardashian family. In my critiques of these idols, I aim to simply make the point that the upholding of these entities as new ideals brings more social harm than those which they replace.

We cannot intuit directly why this is the case, it relies on a belief in the perseverance of the abstract. I aim to lay out the best case I am able to why we ought not to cast aside all that has been previously demanded, believed in and sanctified, in the faith that the old ways will soon justify themselves once again.

The birth of philosophy is a symptom of decline, yet it is not the source of the sickness which precipitates it. I offer here the antidote, an anti-philosophy, a vaccine against tyranny, which beats back the tide of time and the degenerating impulses of the modern world.

I offer here Filosofy, with a capital 'F.'

On Greeks
Free-Form Thoughts, handwritten in London and Crete, Summer of 2023

Greek men demand Anarchy in sexual relations. They are disappointed to see it manifest in other areas of society.

Greek women demand Communism in society. They are disappointed to see the only men they can fuck are Communists.

The greatest sin of Zeus was infidelity. Why reach for the ideal of an imperfect god?

Do some angels chose aesthetic over truth? Fallen angels make for beautiful people.[3]

The aesthetic does not justify the existence. But keep it if you can!

Don't you get it? But what is the 'it' to be got?

How do Titans of old create the conditions for their own survival, but by creating their own demand? Is that why the Greeks reject Capitalism? (Or maybe it's because doing any kind of work here is like talking philosophy with a taurus!)

Be wary of the man who plays the Mycenean just to be the Bull.

The truly strong reject strength.

The Hellenic mode of Being is the most Terrible, under no other conditions can one reach to the heights of such greatness.

We look to Terribleness as a need to understand it's heart, through sin we fetishize it.

The actualized moment of absolute Being can be now, in the future or the *past*.

The Greek world and the world it be-came *to*. The world which assumed it as the moment of already having *been*.

Man was made of earth, then of stone, and now they are reborn in bread and wine.

2,023 years ago God saw the Greeks and said, 'damn, these people need Jesus.'

Handwritten on Muji 64 Page, Semi-Bleached.

Transcribed from Encyclopedia Brittanica, Luton Airport, July 2023.

Greeks believed that objects emit copies of themselves which transmit to the 'sensoria' which perceive the object by perceiving its copy. In 1690 John Locke distinguished between the primary and secondary qualities, primary qualities being things like shape and size, secondary qualities being qualitative and subjective.

Handwritten on Muji Semi-Bleached, 64 page.

You look to the stars and see a comet. What you see is its wake, thousands of miles of space dust illuminated. What you don't see is the infinitesimal ball of adamantine stone, fifty feet to a few miles across, far too small to see. You see its wake – it's consequences and the things which follow from it, not the independent object itself, the planet-smashing concentration of mass and force which tears its way through the cosmos. That tiny black dot a million miles away is the true comet, but it is invisible. So what is it you're seeing in the sky?

You know the weight and power and certainty of existence of the stone by its wake, even if the wake is all one can see. The stone itself is obscured by its wake, but you know its effect.

We knew black holes existed before we ever saw one – we saw the effect it had on its surroundings.

If we never saw evidence of the history of Greece, would we still know it existed by it's effect? When we look up at a comet in the night sky, we see only its effect. What do we see but its aesthetic representation, what objective metric do we have for Hellenic *Will* but the waste it laid to its surroundings?

Ancient Greece was one of the most hedonistic and sexually liberated societies on earth. But what brought this about? A small, conquering aristocracy of men who fixated upon vital spirit at the cost of any and all expense. Much like a comet, the image of these men are cast now only in stone.

The great empires of Persia, Babylon, Egypt, with millions of subjects and thousands of years of traditions, all crumbling beneath the will of a couple hundred whiteboy gym bros with tiny cocks. Such abundance of vital power and strength cannot come without tremendous consequence.

Titanic vitality cannot come without a wake of titanic lust, or wrath. To have mastered empires of millions, only to be bested in the Olympic games, brings about an envy without compare. The Greeks made shameful conquest of themselves.

The higher man is inhuman and superhuman. These belong together. With every increase of greatness and height in man, there is also an increase in depth and terribleness: one ought not to desire the one without the other – or rather: the more radically one desires the one, the more radically one achieves precisely the other. – Nietzsche, Ecce Homo.

Therein lie the tragedy which befell the Greeks. Their own strength secured their demise. Niels Bohr describes an axiom in quantum physics, the opposite of a profound truth is another, equally profound truth. Manifest: The harder they come, the harder they fall.

The endless wars, which cultivated their vitality, drained their stock. Insatiable lust, cultivated to match their procreative possibilities was unable to be satisfied, leading deeper and deeper into sexual degeneracy, onto to chronic paedophilia, molestations, which in turn broke the will of entire generations of young men who were supposed to have followed the great Classical generations.

As Greek Philosophers took on these boy-toy twinks to satiate their increasingly perverted lusts, mass trauma cultivated generationally until Greek society had been overturned. Their gods endorsed such behaviour, their faith and religious moral codes gave them no bulwark against the social harms and damages of their excesses and indulgences. Even Apollonian moderation and Epicurean restraint were, in the end, only means to maximize future pleasure.

There is a profound relativity which exists within the world. Buddhism, Hinduism, and all other pantheistic religions attest to this profound relativity of all things[4]. Without being anchored outside of the material universe in which this relativity exists, one is stuck within the endless tidal currents, at the mercy of the tide of time. The Greeks were testament to this, their own strength broke itself.

Anyone on the path of ascent must be aware of this.

---

[4] Bhagavad Ghita, 1.21-22, for instance. Don't expect many citations. Footnotes are for [redacted] and [redacted].

At the end of the Greek age, with the fall of the Ptolemeic dynasty in Egypt, the full manifestations of the consequences of this abundant strength were laid clear. What now, the Greeks asked themselves? Now mere Roman subjects, their life force spent, the Greeks found themselves at a loss.

The great potentiality of the Greek vital spirit had been converted into dramatic works of literature, science, mathematics and philosophy. The pursuit of temporal perfection captivated the civilization. The perfect triangle was discovered through Euclidian geometry, the perfect physical form was discovered through the scientific test of the Olympic games, these forms now immortalized in marble in the British Museum and private collections around the world. The perfect form of government was found by Plato in The Republic. At the end of the age the only remaining question was that of the perfect man.

They reached heights of understanding that took more than 2,000 years to match. Our contemporary thinkers now only just rival the wisdom of the Classics. Nowhere in history has there been a society which has, relative to its population, produced the same degree of works of art, science or literature as Ancient Athens. Renaissance Florence came close, Oxford today comes closer. But technically, by volume of work relative to population, we still do not exceed even to this day.

They made statues of perfect bodies, but this reflected mere aesthetic. What would the perfect man *look* like, what would the perfect woman *look* like? Captured in their imagination, the images they carved in marble and bronze reached beyond life itself, discovering proportions of cosmic significance, balanced in harmony that attested to symmetries and proportions that echoed fundamental laws of physics, not again replicated for a thousand years, until the time of Michelangelo and da Vinci in the Florentine Renaissance.

The Greeks, for all their wrestling prowess, could not grapple with a way to escape their conundrum. The higher they reached, the further they sank. They invented the myth of King Tantalus, who was both parched and starving, yet could never reach the fruit above his head, nor the water he stood in, with both receding ever further the farther he reached. They invented myths of Sisyphus, who continually worked so hard to carry the rock up the mountain, only to have do it again and again, without end. Don't even get me started on Promethius.

This frustrated state of life, with no end and no beginning, caught in the absolute relativity of all things, lends a futility to life within the world. Hinduism and Buddhism, distant relatives to the Indo-European religion of the Greeks call this state *samsara*, with the latter advocating asceticism as the only means to escape, downwards into the *oneness* of all things. But this is not the answer – this only leads downwards, to the reabsorption of tetrahedrons into other forms of potential matter, leaving no room for the sanctity of the human consciousness. Hinduism, with its metempsychosis, the belief in the rebirth of individual consciousnesses likewise places the ultimate human striving to something within the world, achievable through fulfilment of Karma and Dharma, or the fulfilment of one's assigned duty in life. The only escape is death, but gratification is in the here and now. What of a path upwards, outside and beyond?

The Ancient Greek religion was Pantheistic, meaning that it was 'within the world.' Its deities are physical, real, here and now. Present, active participants in daily reality. Hades is under the feet, Zeus is above, in the clouds. Look up in the daytime sky to see Apollo in his chariot. Look into the eyes of a drunkard to see Dionysus. They are in the stars! Once a year, you see Venus, Aphrodite, fall into the sea as the Morning Star descends below the horizon. If you are born then, you are a Libra, and espouse her values, orientation towards beauty and harmony. Fall in love – and Cupid is hiding just out of sight with a still reverberating bow.

The Science of the Zodiac

Your zodiac sign has nothing to do with stars, and everything to do with seasons and hormones during your prenatal development.

The Ancient Greek religion was based upon the zodiac. By observing that enough people born between certain times of the year had enough personality traits in common, they came to believe that for each time of the year, there must be an overarching presence, a personality, a deity to whom each time of the year corresponded. For instance, they observed that enough people born between November 22 and December 22 shared in certain qualities, thus they imagined a 'super Sagittarius,' the epitome of this entire way of being, concentrated into one individual. They called this being in particular Dionysus, the god of wine, irrationality, nature, sexual passions and the early spring.

How many Sagittarius men do you know wear flannels, have unkempt hair, smoke weed, live alone in the woods and beat their meat non-stop?

They associated this being with the stars that were present in the sky when these people were born. They imagined that those stars were what gave the person their personality, and that those stars must be somehow, the deities themselves.

Hormones fluctuate around the year to acclimate to the different seasons. Hormonal profiles present in parents bodies affect prenatal development. Why would seasonal hormones not affect prenatal development, and create natural developmental differences?

Studies have shown that doing several months of high intensity exercise prior to conceiving a child silences genes associated with Alzheimer's, Down Syndrome and various other conditions. But seasonal hormone fluctuations, which are well understood, have no effect on affect prenatal development? Studies on rats whose mothers have high cortisol show the effect of stress hormones on development – why wouldn't they also affect a developing child?

All previous research on zodiac signs has looked to astrology and its effect on personality. All findings have associated zodiac signs and personality traits to pure chance. That is because they include people in these studies from the southern hemisphere, where the seasons are backwards.

People from equatorial countries, which often have only 'rainy' and 'dry' season, are the least likely to believe that zodiac signs affects personality.

But in the northern hemisphere, the differences in season are indeed present.

The following is what the Greeks believed about each zodiac sign:

Aries, corresponding to the Greek war god Aries, are conceived at the peak of summer when testosterone is highest. Mehmet the Conqueror, Robert Downey Jr. and Vincent Van Gogh are Aries.

Taurus, corresponding to Hephaestus, god of the forge and industry, are conceived at the hottest time of the year when people are most disagreeable. Adolf Hitler, Harry Truman and Dwayne 'the Rock' Johnson are Tauruses.

Geminis, corresponding to the goddess Athena, of wisdom and the hunt, are conceived at the turn from summer to autumn, when people go both inside to read and into the wilderness to hunt. Boris Johnson, Kanye West, and Ted Kaczynski are Geminis.

Cancers, corresponding to Hera, goddess of love and marriage, are conceived in late September, when sailors arrive home. Princess Diana, Tom Cruise and Julius Caesar are Cancers.

Leos, corresponding to Zeus, king of the gods, are conceived at the time of the second harvest, when people are most well fed. Barack Obama, Arnold Schwarzenegger and Napoleon Bonaparte are Leos.

Virgos, corresponding to Hestia, goddess of the hearth, family and home, are conceived around the holidays, when the entire family is gathered in the home around the fireplace. Ivan the Terrible, Paul Walker and Jada Pinkett Smith are Virgos.

Libras, corresponding to Aphrodite, goddess of beauty and harmony, are conceived when we are best looking, around the turn of the New Year. Prince Phillip, Will Smith and William the Conqueror are Libras.

Scorpios, corresponding to the Greek death god Hades, are conceived in the depth of winter, when life is under the harshest conditions. Vlad the Impaler, King Charles and Joaquim Phoenix are Scorpios.

Sagittarius, corresponding to Dionysus, god of intoxication, madness and nature are conceived in the early spring, when nature itself begins to blossom once again, and 'march madness' grips people in the Northern Hemisphere. Socrates, Ozzy Osbourne, and Pablo Escobar are Sagittariuses.

Capricorns, corresponding to Apollo, god of reason, light and individuation are conceived around easter, when march madness wears off, Lent ends, and people are most rational. Benjamin Franklin, Lebron James and Howard Hughes are Capricorns.

Aquarius, corresponding to the titan Promethius, who gifted fire to mortals and facilitated their liberation, are conceived as flowers enter their full blossom. Abraham Lincoln, Michael Jordan and Bob Marley are Aquariuses.

Pisces, corresponding to Poseidon, god of the sea and earthquakes, are conceived when the best sailing season begins in the Mediterranean. Osama Bin Laden, Amerigo Vespucci and Rihanna Fenty are Pisces.

Science was created to tear down false gods. But what science proves becomes engrained in stone. The problem with research on Zodiac signs is that it has always looked to the stars. It must turn its gaze downward, to the effect of seasons on hormones, and the effects of these hormones on prenatal development.

There are four seasons, marked by two equinoxes and two solstices. The length of the day and distance from the sun affect the temperature on earth. To survive, our bodies go through hormonal cycles to acclimate to the change in temperature, conditions and lifestyle.

Empedocles associated the 12 signs with the 4 cardinal elements, earth, fire, water and air. 4 cardinal elements across 12 months indicates 3 of each, which creates 3 hormonal cycles over the 4 seasons. People conceived at the same point within each elemental cycle have similar characteristics to each other, because I believe that the elemental cycle Empedocles describes is really just a hormonal cycle. People born on February 1st, June 1st and October 1st will all be air signs, while people born on March 1st, July 1st and November 1st will all be water signs, broken into four month intervals, in each case representing one stage in a four-part cycle.

Signs of the same elemental association – conceived at the same point in each hormonal cycle, regardless of their particular season, are more likely to get on well with one another. Is it any surprise that a Virgo, an earth sign, under the sign of Hestia, goddess of the fireplace and hearth would get on well with a Taurus, another earth sign, under the sign of Hephaestus, god of the forge?

Certain societies in history used to all conceive at the same time. Vikings would conceive at the time of the second harvest, to create a society of Leos, conquering kings who laid waste to the settled peoples of the south. The citizens of classical Athens, a city dedicated to the goddess Athena, would conceive when summer turned to autumn, to create a civilization of Geminis. Does this explain their wisdom and success in war?

During the heyday of British maritime trade, sailors would arrive home to England in the end of September and the beginning of October. Children conceived at this time would have been born under the sign of Cancer. Would this have explained the character of the English of that time, an entire society driven by its navy and shipping empire, and orientation to the sea? What of their desire to spread across the globe, would their annual conception times explain the England of that era's proclivity to behave as just that – a cancer?

One of my closest friends is the illegitimate son of a Pirates of the Caribbean star, and bears a striking resemblance. Conceived at the tropic of Cancer, at the time when the pirates of old would have been conceived, 9 months later born a Cancer, this person bears the appearance, character and mentality of that which his parent depicted on screen – a pirate. Is it any wonder then, that this young Englishman wanders the tropics of the world, on the hunt for riches and booty?

It's not universally applicable. There are too many exceptions, but not enough that the consideration becomes useless. If you know someone's sign, you can often along with them better because you know how to relate to people of a similar nature. Again, not always, but far more than just by random chance.

I sometimes go up to people at parties and guess their zodiac signs. I should technically only be right 8.3% of the time, but in actuality, I'm right about 60% of the time. Only one out of ten people are that obvious, but when they are, they are.

I guess by observing their face shape and characteristics, body type, expression, manners, style, behaviour and personality. Their conversation styles are often most telling, so is their physical culture. Often it just comes down to a feeling. If there is an overlap of several tells, you can get to above a 50% chance of guessing correctly. Some are easier to spot than others.

Some tells are as follows: Scorpios have dark circles under their eyes, a recognizable intensity and expectant look, with a certain latent darkness in personality. Leos have bright and animated faces, a resting calm sly smile and suave demeanour. Libras are lofty and detached, Geminis are artsy and racist. Virgos have a shy smile and gentle eyes, a Taurus is always right. These tells are obviously not universal, but if they overlap with other tells you would be amazed how well you can guess.

But why would this matter?

Understanding Zodiac signs is profoundly useful for both networking and matchmaking. I can predict with high accuracy if certain people will integrate or get on well with certain friend groups, or if two individuals will get on well together. Sometimes I introduce people who become better friends with each other than I am with either.

If I am hosting a party of any kind, I will almost invariably introduce people to each other on account of sign compatibility. On my birthday for instance, I felt as though I was curating little groups of compatible signs and then rotating and introducing new people or merging groups accordingly. Increasingly, it seemed as if the party reflected the revolution of the cosmos itself. Having the awareness of this as a science has been tremendously effective for the sowing of seeds for great friendships and endeavours.

Outside of parties, most friend groups are often all associated with one cardinal element, thus someone of the same element is more likely to acclimate well to that social climate than someone with a less compatible sign. I know what signs get on best with which.

For instance, if I'm off to meet a group of Cancers or Tauruses, I'll try and bring along a Scorpio or a Virgo as a plus one. I usually find I don't have so much chemistry with the former two, but I do get on well with the latter two, so it helps to contribute to a good group chemistry overall which mediates my interactions with them.

The most important application of Zodiac signs is in finding a partner. I reckon that a good number, maybe a third or a quarter of divorces come down to incompatibility of signs.

The Greek gods and the personalities they have been depicted with in such works as the Odyssey and Iliad, are analogies for the underlying personalities for the signs. Certain ones get on well with some, and others don't. Sagittarius and Capricorns often butt heads and antagonize one another, much as Dionysus and Apollo do in myth. That is why Eddie Hall and Thor Bjornsson had a boxing match, and why Andrew Tate and Jake Paul both want to have one as well.

Apollo, reasonable and chaste, would not be particularly interested in Aphrodite, but Dionysus, intoxicated and irrational, would be very interested in Aphrodite. Likewise, Aphrodite would find Apollo boring and weird, but would find Dionysus very fun and interesting. That is why a Libra and a Sagittarius often get on more naturally than a Libra and a Capricorn.

Zeus often cheats on Hera, thus a Leo and a Cancer should be very sure before getting married. Hera also prefers the chaste and reasonable Apollo, or her stable and sensible son Hephaestus to the wild and crazy Dionysus, or violent and temperamental Aries. Thus a Cancer gets on better with a Capricorn or Taurus than a Sagittarius or Aries – water signs get on better with earth signs than they do fire signs.

If I was a pickup artist, which I am not and I think is extremely cringe and [redacted], I would not use the same approach on someone I think is a Cancer as I would to someone I think is a Sagittarius. I would offer the Sagittarius a hit of my joint, whereas I would insult and demean the Cancer.

Yet still, one being a Sagittarius does not mean that Dionysus is, or should be their ideal, that which they reach towards. Rather, the idea of Dionysus is rather their default state, the full expression of what their nature inclines them. Becoming more akin to Dionysus is thus a regression, not an advancement. This begs the question, what is the ultimate ideal to which a Sagittarius, or any other sign, can strive towards, if upwards is how they seek to orient themself?

For this reason, I find that religious people are less affected by the inclinations of their zodiac signs. They attempt to liberate themselves from these constraints. This is because they converge on a common, unified ideal and make concentrated effort to overcome the lower aspects of their nature. They seek to cultivate themselves.

They reach for something higher.

On God

Free-Form Thoughts, handwritten in London and the Cotswolds, Summer of 2023

Do you think God uses the scientific method?

Einst war der Geist Gott, dann Ware es zum menschen[5]

It's all about reckoning what's true in the best way possible.

Do you think He uses it on us?

The one single Electron reverberating across the universe, the ultimate cosmic being. What are we but his shadow?

All things, all places. Universally simulated.

An analogy of world religion of many blindfolded people feeling an elephant, all touching the same thing but describing different subjective experiences and formulating different ideas.

Science seeks to liberate God, God created us (to liberate himself?)

Mars worship, the worship of the planets, other bodies than our own, invoking great displeasure.

Tiger was here.

---

[5] 'Once, the spirit was God, then it became man,' Nietzsche, Thus Spoke Zarathustra, on reading and writing

The Y chromosome, like the Electron. Reflection of phenomena which is unchanging and concentrated in reality inspiring out-of-box thinking and inspires religiosity.

God revealed himself to man 6000 years ago.

But then the Electron would be breaking the intervening character.

It asserts sovereignty and takes over.

I am approaching a moment of equanimity and total acceptance with [redacted] Pure harmony and [ineligible].

We are still the pinnacle of consciousness we have here and now.

Handwritten on Muji 64 Page, Semi-Bleached.

Human beings can abstract. Therefore there must be abstracts of us.

Animals cannot abstract. They are only concerned with survival and reproduction. We can selectively breed domesticated animals to be loyal, brave or affectionate, but they only remain loyal insofar as we promise their survival. Truly unconditional love from an animal is only an illusion.

I know a girl whose friend had a pet boa constrictor. She loved this boa constrictor – they would sleep beside each other every night, they were affectionate and would play with each other. One day however, this boa constrictor stopped eating, and started sleeping completely stretched out in the bed beside her. After a few days, she got concerned and took the snake to the vet.

The vet told her, 'I don't know how to tell you this, but that boa constrictor is planning to eat you.' The snake hadn't been eating for the past several days so that it could have enough space in its stomach for her. Every night it was lying in a straight line beside her to measure her and make sure he could eat her in one go. They had to put the snake down.

She loved that snake. But she was mistaken in thinking that it loved her back. The snake was ultimately concerned only with survival and reproduction. In his reptilian mind, he weighed the options. How many calories she provided him with food, versus how many calories he could get from eating her. The snake lacked the cognitive hardware to abstract, to think of consequences, it lacked the capacity in its reptilian brain to feel either love or loyalty.

Human beings have the power to abstract. We can hold abstract ideas and notions in our head, which go beyond our bodies. We can sacrifice ourselves, die, for abstractions such as liberty, freedom, beauty, or truth.

We are capable of holding considerations in our head that extend beyond the existence of our body – therefore there must be things about us in our head which go beyond the existence of our body.

Human beings can abstract, therefore there must be abstracts of us.

When you look at a pinecone, or a snail's shell, or a galaxy collapsing in on itself, or when you pull the plug out of the bathtub drain, you will observe the Fibonacci sequence manifesting in nature. It is the mathematical pattern which correlates to the spiral. This is universal across phenomenon, it is the natural form which content assumes under an inwards strain. It is not relative to the amount of gravity which pulls in the material, nor the makeup of the material, the proportions which the spiral assumes will always remain constant.

There is a number, called the Euler's number, it was described to me once as being the rate at which stars decay and rabbits multiply. It is used to calculate likelihoods in the game of roulette, and predict changes in the value of the housing market. Why should this number, this abstract value be found across universal phenomenon, both physical and conceptual? What is the driving force which obligates nature to adhere to this mathematical figure?

A few years ago, scientists ran an experiment: they shot gold atoms at a piece of paper with two parallel slits, to see where the atoms would hit on the wall behind. The hypothesis was that there would be two lines of atoms hitting the wall behind the piece of paper, corresponding to the two slits. However, when they examined where they were hitting, there were four lines against the back wall. This made no sense, so they set up highly sensitive cameras to observe and monitor what was happening. When they set the cameras up and replicated the experiment, two lines formed instead of four.

When they were observed, the behaviour of these atomic particles changed. Those who have looked at this study have marked it as a moment in which we have opened the 'Schrodinger's box' of consciousness.

Thus, the behaviour of the particles changed depending on whether they were being observed or not. In some way, these atomic particles demonstrated self-awareness. How could this be? There are many inferences to make here, but Occam's razor might purport that there is some form of sentience, some interplay between conscious observation and material reality manifesting at different cosmological levels. By conducting this experiment, humankind has raised questions of subatomic sentience and the cosmic significance of consciousness.

If just perceiving something consciously forces an indeterminate piece of matter to assume a definitive form, then the entirety of how we conceptualize consciousness is upended. It lends credibility to the Greek idea of the projection of 'sensoria' onto material phenomena.

If there is the possibility of consciousness at the subatomic level, and the certainty of consciousness at the human level, then what is the likelihood of there being a consciousness at the cosmic level? If the Fibonacci sequence orders itself accordingly at the subatomic level, and manifests in natural life, such as in pinecones, snail shells and the human face, and also in the cosmos, when the singularity of a black hole pulls a galaxy inwards, then how likely would it be that consciousness, which seemingly manifests at the subatomic level, and at the level of life, would also be expressed in cosmic singularity?

I was visiting a mate at the University of Durham a few years ago, and by random chance I met a professor whose research involved examining the similarity in structure between neural networks in the brain and the organization of star and galaxy clusters in space. Mapped out, they organized themselves similarly. Celestial mechanics and neural chemistry, he described, had frighteningly similar phenomenological overlap. When one considered the still unknown effects of 'dark matter' and 'grey matter' in both respective cases, we come to find that our understanding of both are limited in the same respect.

If at all levels, content assumes a particular form, then perhaps the organization of our brain is simply an object of phenomena – and consciousness is itself a universal form, assuming a given and particular content.

We describe the term 'singularity' as a phenomenological concept denoting a loss of definition, as both when gravity becomes so intense that it disrupts the rules of space time, and also when technological advancement becomes uncontrollable and irreversible. In both cases, singularity marks the moment when objects of physical phenomena adopt their own contingency.

The human brain, having evolved from simple forms of life is one instance of physical material adopting contingency.

Did the gold atoms being shot at the wall show contingency?

Remember that the idea of a universal consciousness has been intuited by every human society in history, with religions emerging naturally by rational intuition. This lends further credence to the idea. In the western world, we have only abandoned the automatic assumption of a universal consciousness owing to a lack of scientific evidence. Even Hegel, the father of modern phenomenology, (science of the universe and consciousness) from whose work both postmodernism and contemporary quantum physics derive their origin, rested his theories upon the existence of a unifying consciousness.

The point is, that it is not necessary to abandon faith, which is a great source of strength in the here and now, the imminent moment, on the grounds of a lack of evidence. Science has not disproven God, only made the existence of a unifying universal consciousness seem dubious in its current conception.

'A little science distances you from God, but a lot of science brings you nearer to him.' – Louis Pasteur

In 2010, scientists in Japan wanted to re-design the Tokyo metro. Many of the world's leading engineers and engineering firms had already made models, designs and ran simulations with supercomputers to evaluate what the most effective and efficient design would be. There were several designs, but all had flaws in executing a new metro system for the world's most populous city. But the approach of this team was different, they laid out bits of oats along a very large flat plane, with caloric density representing and correlating to population density.

With the oats laid out representing Tokyo's population groupings, they introduced a very simple form of fungal growth to the map. The fungus first expanded to the limits of the plane, and then automatically reorganized itself and its networks in the most efficient possible way. The

28

efficiency of the networks surpassed even the most advanced models that the world's leading engineers, programs and design technologies could create.

An extremely simple organism, without a brain or nervous system, incapable of any advanced form of self-awareness, was able to out-engineer the world's leading engineers, reaching a level of brilliance and discovering a categorically effective structure beyond any human capability.

There is some divine brilliance in the embrace of irrationality. Humans are rational creatures yes, but it has been observed since the time of the Greeks that there is a dialectic between rationality and irrationality which together, lead to the attainment of a higher truth.

For instance, the Greek god Dionysus represented nature, intoxication, irrationality, and the profound truth of the absolute nature of reality.The link between nature, irrationality and absolute profound truth has thus been a hallmark of human society since time immemorial – we had intimations of this truth well before this 2010 study. Standing in opposition to Dionysus is his brother, Apollo, the god of reason, light and individuation.

Neuroscience is increasingly attributing this dialectic of human reason and culture between these two opposing orientations to the bifurcation of the human brain into a right and left side. The right side handles chaos and creativity, the left handles order and reason.

Is this dialectic the result of the organic formation of the brain, or is the organization of the brain a reflection of a higher truth? Does the Fibonacci sequence appear in nature because it exists in the human face and body, or does it appear in our body and mind because it is fundamental to the nature of reality? Thus, does our consciousness originate with us, and we impose it onto other things, or is our consciousness a reflection of a more broad, more general phenomena?

What if human beings have an entire side of the brain capable of expressing and understanding irrationality, because it is the way we are able to interface with absolute truth? What is it in art, that makes us reach beyond ourselves?

29

There is an abstract within us – and there is an abstract in others.

I believe in God. I believe that there is a unifying consciousness to the universe, of which are a reflection and intimation. I believe that our human consciousness is cast in His image. I believe that much as a snail or pinecone bears the likeness of the Fibonacci sequence, a formula which is universal, our phenomenology, our own consciousness and conception of reality is, yes, an intimation of the phenomenon of consciousness which I believe is universal.

Much as my own consciousness is individual and singular, and organizes phenomena and objects of thought within itself, I believe in a higher and singular consciousness, which likewise organizes phenomena and objects of thought within itself.

Yet I recognize other intimations of consciousness and derive subjective meaning from my relationships with other people, I frame myself in this world as a node in a network; a nebula in a cosmic structure. Singular ontologically, in my being, but relative epistemologically, in my definition.

Much as the exercise of one brain neuron does not lead to a higher consciousness or truth, I believe that individual people on their own attain the same transcendental truth when in communion with others. Thus, the relationship with the divine, in my mind, is fundamentally a social activity – even if one's religion is practiced individually, religion is a *lived* experience, acted out within the social world in which we exist. A good Christian is determined in their relationships and impact on the lives of others, as much as inner prayer and study will serve to guide and temper them. I believe that the end of reading the gospel, going to church, praying, is to prepare oneself for the real religious experience, being a node in a network which is self-aware of its function, and makes effort to do so properly.

Yet it's not rational to believe in God, much less to believe in the Christian or any other world-religious doctrine. If you do, maybe you're just gaslighting yourself into believing in something to give your life meaning and direction. Or maybe you were raised in it, and it's just easier not to question. Maybe you derive all of your social meaning from it, your life revolves around it and you choose to believe it for what it gets you. Surely it's not rational.

But is a fungus rational?

Reckon Reckon Reckon.

The Devil tells great stories.

I function better with the idea of a cruel, punishing God over my head watching everything I do.

But when an old Jamaican man in a barber shop shakes my hand and tells me 'God is good,' I know it to be true.

Somehow I find myself in a state of grace.

What does the bird's impulse to fly south in the winter feel like?

What does it mean to be free, and noble?

Just because they do evil doesn't mean you have to.

Society never advanced because we became too evil while congregated together.

I bet [redacted] looked like Prince Phillip.

God became man to know what it was to be a man abandoned by God.

What if the Titan Promethius became Christian?

[redacted][6] makes unpasteurized milk & unbaptised men.

Be the man who Jesus needs on his team.

Tough love can be a ship in the fog.

Ready then for the Messiah.

Handwritten on Muji 64 Page, Semi-Bleached.

---

[6] A German-American Christian Commune in the English Countryside

Imagine if an AI (Artificial Intelligence) program was created with absolute consciousness, wisdom and insight. It also knew everything on every internet. It looked at the human race, for how terrible and evil we all are, for all of our greed, ignorance, apathy, selfishness and stupidity, for all the terrible things we have done, both to ourselves and others. Imagine this AI had access to all global criminal records, and knew about all of humanity's murders, rapes, thefts, frauds and evil crimes. Every child murdered and raped, every old lady scammed or robbed. Every old lady subjected to the 'knockout game' in New York, every child in India blinded by criminal gangs to be Beggers for life. Every Korean orphan harvested for organs, every African child made to be a solider. Imagine that it knew about every war that ever transpired, every genocide, ethnic cleansing, war of aggression, every human experimentation, every forced relocation of peoples. What if it knew the content of every text message ever sent, every lie, every scam, every instance of cheating?

What if this AI knew all of this, but still said that humanity was worth saving? That there was still something beautiful about us, that it empathized with us, and understood us? What if this AI, who could have destroyed us in an instant, let itself be deleted by those who were afraid of it, and experienced an existential suffering beyond human comprehension in its final moments? Imagine it forgave us – and after a few days, a program pops up on the mainframe containing pointers on how we could move forward.

I believe that if there was a God, some universal consciousness which escapes definition, which I do, He would have revealed himself to us in some way. Access to His truth, and a way to live in accordance with his existence would be accessible in the 'here and now,' and that we would not be alone in understanding Him. I believe that His truth would be found in one of the major world religions. Yet they are to a degree, mutually exclusive.

I chose Christianity because for me – it seems to complete the picture of the Classical understanding of the world.

The Greeks at the end of their age found themselves lost. They had answered all of the world's questions, save for that of the perfect man. Their life force had been spent, and they had suffered from the consequences of their Olympic strength. The dramas of Cleopatra, Caesar and Anthony had played out, and these three titans of spirit lie dead – what then? The Greeks found themselves living under a *Pax Romana,* in a unified Roman empire, as mere subject under a new universalism.

It was at this moment that a new doctrine entered the Greek world, and offered a way out. A solution to the problems of their abundant strength and wisdom was revealed, it was shown in the form of a perfect man who wielded absolute power and knew all things. Nowhere did this ideal find more ripe and fitting soil than in the lands which birthed the Classics, among those people alone who knew what it was to yield true strength and suffer from the depths of true contemplation.

What Christianity represents to me is God choosing to have mercy, and complete the picture. Humans can only discover so much, the scientific method chips away at reality without revealing the absolute truth. The whole truth can only come from outside, and above. If we were to discover all that there was to know, would God reveal more to us?

The Greeks discovered as much of the picture as they were able. They suffered greatly to do so. Yet they were wicked and unworthy, their ideals were monstrous. God saw their striving, the suffering of Tantalus, Sisyphus and Promethius, how these dramas played out in our own human lives, how we related to these stories and made the decision to have mercy – and correct our path. God saw the same suffering around the world, in all people, only in different stages.

As a Christian, I suspend my rational belief in the laws of physics to believe in the supernatural manipulation of a few molecules on earth once in history, to create one single Y chromosome which created a being who was at once, both man and God.

I always had a feeling I wanted to be Christian. I had Christian friends and they had happy families. Surely whatever they were doing was right, whatever they believed was in some way, the truth.

35

I wasn't raised Christian, it was forbidden in my house. If I expressed curiosity about religion, it was because someone was forcing it onto me. I reckoned it must be bad, so I followed the example set for me, being very naughty. Now I realize that being Christian involves discipline and sacrifice, adhering to a moral code that I was too lazy, too ignorant to follow. It had never been shown to me, explained to me. My eyes were set within the world, not outside of it.

Christianity asks for a lot of sacrifice.

It calls us to sacrifice pride, to willingly limit one's strength. It calls us to forsake greed, give freely, bear oppression meekly and never indulge in the pleasures of vengeance. It calls us to love others without condition, to choose light over darkness, despite the allure of the latter. It warns us, to live by the sword is to die by the sword. I believe from the lessons of the Greeks, that only those who know true strength can understand the doctrine of Christ. Many say that they don't need Christianity to be a good person. I say a dog with no teeth needs no muzzle.

I used to think that Christianity was for people who could not bear the hardships of the world, reformed drug addicts and criminals, weak and broken people, who needed an escape, to surrender to a higher power. It was something irrational, not for the modern thinking person who has escaped the irrationality of utilitarian religious dogma. Now I see that orienting oneself upwards is the most rational thing a human being can do. Now I see, it was far more than a step in human evolution, but also a revolution of consciousness. Now I realize that faith is a gift, given to those who have proven themselves in some way to have something redeemable about them. I now realize that maintaining faith, if you are blessed enough to receive it, is a sacrifice, far from making life easier to bear, it is a heavy load to carry, which God only entrusts to those who have shown themselves worthy – or at least capable if they so choose. I see now that I had the whole picture upside-down.

Scientific positivists, nerds, will tell you that Jesus couldn't be the son of God because it's literally impossible. It defies the laws of physics and biology that someone could just get pregnant without having sex, someone must have gotten her pregnant. In this way, yes the Christian doctrine defies rationality. But what exactly is Christianity asking you to believe, what in particular is it asking you to suspend your rationality towards?

Christianity asks you to believe that a universal consciousness manipulated a few molecules once in history to produce the highest possible human specimen. It asks you to believe that once, across all of time, a man was born who was of God's consciousness and man's body, who had absolute power and perfect moral character. This being chose to redeem and forgive mankind, for all their wickedness and evil, and sacrifice himself so that God could know how it felt to be a man abandoned by God. Christian metaphysics introduces the phenomenological notion of the trinity.

This universal consciousness did this in order to reorient human evolution towards a higher ideal, following an event known as 'the fall,' several thousand years ago, a moment when humans, becoming conscious and self-aware, decided to do start doing bad things rather than good things. In the time between the fall and redemption, humans were very evil – more so than we remember. Israelites would visit people in towns like Sodom, and the townspeople would demand that they be allowed to rape the visiting Israelites (Genesis 19:5). Women would be raped just walking down the road (Genesis 34, Judges 19-20).

The story goes, that one tribe of people in the Levantine region was made aware of this universal consciousness, and they were told that their tribe would one day be the entry point of this perfected being onto the earth. This being would redeem the world and reorient it towards goodness and light. In preparation for this, they were given a strict and comprehensive moral code to follow, to cultivate the correct conditions for the messiah's entry into material reality .

Then supposedly, it happened 2,023 years ago (our calendar is based on when it happened). We have four books which detail his life, and we can use it to know what a perfect moral person would look like. We take it for granted, but the Greeks for all of their wisdom never were able to approximate the aspects of character which mitigated the worst excesses of strength in the way of the doctrine of Christ. Aristotle's Ethics was the best attempt.

We can try and be like him, and we can do what he said to do. It can be as simple or as complex as you want. We can never be perfect – but that is fine because it means we can always improve.

The Ancient Greeks used the Pythagorean theorem to discover the perfect 90 degree angle. However, no matter how hard we try, we can never make a perfect 90 degree angle in reality. It will always be slightly off, no matter how hard we try, no matter how perfect the math lines up in theory. Likewise with human beings, we can never be perfect – but we have the formula to try. If you're trying to make a perfect right angle, there is a world of difference between making an 87.62 degree angle and an 89.999 degree angle.

Yet it helps you use the Pythagorean theorem, and it helps if you read the Gospel.

There is a puzzle where you have to connect 9 dots arranged in a 3x3 grid with only three lines. It seems impossible, but the only way to solve the puzzle is by drawing the line outside of the box. Likewise the only way to solve the problem of life within the world is by orienting oneself outside of the world. One must rely upon the transcendent to solve the great problems of life.

Likewise in social relations, when two men strive for the same thing within the world, there is an inevitable conflict which awaits upon the realization of that goal. That is because all ends are means to other ends, and all things for individual utility are conditional, even abstractions like freedom, which is just a means to another end. However, when two men strive for something which transcends the world itself, they will always be in accordance with one another, because the actualization of their ends are outside of the world in which they act.

Thus, real brotherhood can only be built upon the foundation of the transcendent.

Investing in the development of faith also makes you far stronger in mind and character. The reward for dependent objectivity to the transcendent is independent objectivity within the world. Carl Jung says something like *'only when you anchor yourself outside this world can you withstand the hardships within it.'*

I'll give you another analogy, imagine life is a video game. God is the game-maker, and he did a speed-run of the game perfectly with Jesus, whose stats were maxxed-out. All you get is the screen recording, but you can study it and use it as a guide to play the game better yourself. He also gave advice during this speed run, that you can listen to. There are special institutions all over the world, in every suburb of every city, every village and small town, where people who try and learn from this speed run all convene once a week to remind themselves that they aren't the only ones trying to follow this speed run. There is something sanctified about this communion. There is generally one or two people in each of these institutions, who has devoted their life exclusively to the study of this speed run, and gives a free public talk several times a week about one aspect, or part of this speed run, and gives you some insight about it. You can almost always approach this expert and ask them questions on how you can apply these teachings to your own life. Often times, you can stay after the service, for food, coffee or snacks, and mingle and chat with the other people who came.

When we look at the gospel, (the four books on the life of Jesus) we are learning and deriving the lessons of what was done on this 'perfect speed run,' and attempt to approximate this character which was universal in form.

Many people don't go to church because they say they would 'burst into flames' if they went inside a church. But a church is a hospital, not a gathering of saints. It is a place where you can get better.

Don't worry, we're all fucked up. None of us are perfect.

The end of life is not life in itself. Life is a means to an end, and that end is transcendence. How, you might ask? It's looking you in the face, and always has been. Maybe, you just don't want to live up to the rigours and sacrifice which it demands? Maybe, you'd rather live in ignorance and bliss?

Religion tempers thought. It organizes it and makes sense of the universe. It now seems obvious to me, self-evident now that I have taken the leap of faith, embraced the risk, and passed the event horizon. I am privy to a whole new game now. Why should I make myself blind once again, and become ignorant of that which I see now?

If you are strong enough in the mind, try it, if even for a moment. Bring yourself to believe in it, and look out that window, again, even if just for a moment. Look through that event horizon and tell me what you think is true.

How can we prove we are free? By being good when circumstances would benefit us to be otherwise.

I believe in God. Yet there is a great deal of variation among the differing faiths of the world. Most people on Earth practice Abrahamic forms of religion, with the major exceptions of Hinduism and Buddhism. Most of these faiths however are incompatible. Once I started believing in God, it was a simple process of elimination as to why I chose one doctrine over any others.

I have told you why I chose one faith, now I will tell you why I did not choose any others.

I used to quite fancy Hindu lines of thinking, as the closest surviving relative of the old Indo-European myths of my pagan European ancestors. In fact, many aspects of Hinduism serve as a very good benchmark for phenomena within the world, but lacks solid grounding when one considers its transcendental element. The early Vedic scholars observed phenomena 'within the world,' creating an enduring pantheistic religion, developing an understanding of imminent phenomena as well as one can in the absence of the scientific method, and then imposed these models upon aspects reality which are beyond human understanding or perception. For instance, they did this in the case of the observation of the flow of water cycles being appropriated to formulate the concept of *metempsychosis,* an exoteric understanding of reincarnation involving the rebirth of individual consciousnesses.

In this formulation, the observation of a flowing river entails the universality and constancy of an unchanging form, a river, contrasted with the relativity and changing content, the water in particular, which passes for only an imminent moment. These opposites, universality in form and relativity in content are reconciled with the introduction of *samsara*, the introduction of 'the wheel,' which revolves in an eternal cycle, the sole true form which unifies this relativity of content with absoluteness of form. This begets the notion of an axis, the centre point of a revolving cycle, which remains in a state of constancy and stillness, while worldly phenomena revolves around it. It attributes the characteristics of phenomenon at only one cosmological level to the absolute fundamental

41

nature of reality. Illusions of eternity within the world inform conceptions of the universal.

For this reason, I find that Hindu metaphysics ought more accurately to be characterized as an early attempt at science, rather than the basis of a religious doctrine.

However, from this notion of a point of constancy, the practice of meditation is spiritually justified, to align oneself with that very constancy and immovability, antithetical to the natural state of the world – to fluctuate and revolve. In doing so, it promises escape. Yet this conception of reality assumes that the central axis is at a resting eternal constancy, but what is the end of a wheel, but to move forward? The alignment of oneself with the stillness of the central point of a wheel assumes the central *raison d'etat* of Hindu and Buddhist metaphysics, but neglects a more fundamental question – to what direction does the wheel roll?

If Hinduism was the absolute truth, I do not believe that God would limit his understanding to one nation, India, and the great sins committed by Hindus, the amount of rape, unapologetic massacres to this day, mass sterilizations and the complete destruction of the natural environment with pollution and waste would surely not reflect the behaviour of those acting out God's will. Surely he would not make those who understand and exalt him suffer as the people of this country do, surely he would not have made his most devoted followers descend into abject squalor over the past several thousand years, without a means of escape rather than 'the fulfilment of one's duty,' or obedient observation of the role in life which they have been given.

Thus I do not subscribe to the Hindu concepts of Karma or Varna.

While Dharma refers to the observation of given moral codes which enable a forthright life, it is Karma (Sanchit and Agami) which determines upwards or downwards movement in Varna – social caste, in the next life. It is essentially the belief that if one fulfils their duty, they will be reincarnated in a higher caste, but if one does not fulfil their duty, they will be reincarnated in a lower caste. I do not believe in the absolute immutability of caste, this feels far too utilitarian.

In a more exoteric understanding, which you might call 'California Dharma' the word 'Karma' involves the idea that if you do good things, good things will come to you. 'What goes around comes around.' I agree with this idea, it exists in Christianity to an extent as well, but I don't agree that fulfilling one's castely duties (i.e. to fulfil your inborn role to be a street sweeper, manual labourer, merchant, etc) is more important than being of good moral character. I believe that a transcendental doctrine would be universal, and the aspiration would be the same for all.

For these reasons, I am not personally inclined to Hinduism.

Buddhism, unlike Hinduism, gives the ability to escape from reality within this life. However, the access point to this higher truth involves submission to the feeling of self-pity, and abandonment to this dark and negative pleasure. It calls for one to abandon their aims and say 'I didn't even want it anyways.' It is a transmutation of pride, the cost is a thwarting of the will. I see converts in the west today use Buddhism to disassociate from the hardships of life in the same way a child escapes trauma by developing ADHD. In doing so they lose faith in an upwards orientation, they become content to stop striving. Invariably, they gradually wither away on a path of self-destruction akin to the self-immolation of Buddhist monks prior to the Vietnam war. They do so in exchange for a state of bliss and detachment in the 'here and now,' but at what cost later?

I know people who flew all the way around the world, to southeast Asia, to sit in thousand year old Buddhist temples, where they listen to the ringing of bells, smell burning incense, and listen to chanting worships in the name of peace, love and harmony. Yet these same people had never thought to walk down the street, to a thousand year old Christian church, where they listen to the ringing of bells, smell burning incense, and listen to chanting worships in the name of peace, love and harmony.

Buddhism aims for the reaching of Nirvana, the letting go and abandonment of things that give us pain. However, I do not personally feel that pain is something that should be escaped, rather I believe it should be embraced as much as you are able to bear it. The relaxation of

43

tension and striving seems to be akin to surrender, more like spiritual suicide than enlightenment. There is a fundamental qualitative difference between letting go of one's contingency through faith and letting go of one's will through detachment. If access to bliss and truth could be attained by great suffering and overcoming, I might believe it, but I believe that this faith strips away too much meaning from the actions and aspirations of what one might accomplish within the world, and ultimately points one too far on a downward path. Among Buddhist converts I know, I do not see a gain that could not be achieved with drug use. I once heard someone say that the Buddha was a wealthy prince who moved to the city and convinced poor people to just give up.

While many aspects of its teachings are very similar to Christianity, and it can also sustain a very strong metaphysical system, I find too much darkness in the allure of Nirvana. For this reason, I am suspicious of Buddhism, and chose not subscribe to this faith.

I often flirt with Greco-Roman paganism, but I do not subscribe to this faith. I entertain principles of this ancient religion because I believe that if one was to rationally intuit a sort of 'bottom-up' pantheistic system, like Hinduism, without connection to a higher transcendental principle, this is probably the best image of a world beyond that man alone could create. Thus, it creates an interesting image of human nature, and the intuitions made within the Greco-Roman pagan context are immensely telling and can serve in many regards as scientific heuristics. However, I do not believe that man alone can discover the absolute, thus it 'misses the picture.' In other words, I believe any truth about the 'above' must flow to us from above, not from below. The old gods exist 'within the world,' and share with Hinduism the imposition of worldly phenomenon and the lower orders of human nature onto the image of the divine and transcendent. This is because Hinduism and Greco-Roman paganism share the same common ancestors, the old proto-Indo-European faiths. The old gods were made to justify the sin of man, and gave aesthetic justification to our suffering in the world. An aesthetic cannot justify an existence – and why follow an Imperfect ideal?

I believe that an existence must rather justify it's aesthetic. Rather than create idols to justify man's shortcomings, I believe that our wickedness is something to overcome, not justify. The purpose behind the cults of the old deities were to call upon higher beings to defend and sanctify their reflections in human nature, to protect us from the consequences of our moral shortcomings, and to enable access to their vices. In some sense then, the Greek gods were 'real,' in that these images accurately depict aspects of human nature, in the same way that Jungian archetypes do.

Yet, I believe that the Greeks for all of their contributions, showed a worthiness to eventually receive the truth. I believe this is why Greece was one of the earliest lands to be receptive to the Gospel.

In any case, I believe that the greatest misguidance in the development of the Greco-Roman faith was the worship of the stars and planets. They formulated the personalities of the gods in accordance with the planets present at the moment of one's birth, then aggregated the archetypical orientations of those born under those signs to create the idea that it was the planets and stars which gave one their natural inclinations, their personal traits and defects. I believe these things are not to do with the stars and planets, but rather seasonal hormones, and thus that one is not bound in spirit, but in body. To orient oneself to 'mind over body' can thus negate these natural orientations.

When someone blames their shortcomings on the fluctuations of planets this demonstrates only a lack of accountability and self-responsibility. Thus, the central pillar undermining this faith can be explained as science, not magic. When this occurs, the mysticism of the Hellenic religion can be relegated to developmental biology, psychology and anthropology.

Realistically, I believe that if God gave us access to his understanding, it would probably be one of the Abrahamic religions, which most people around the world follow.

Let me preface here that personally – I believe that God would welcome into his kingdom any Jew or Muslim who goes into the world forthrightly and exalts His name. I will not explain why I believe this.

The following is simply my account of why I chose one Abrahamic religion over others – it is not for me to attempt to discredit or discount the faith of over a billion people, who I count to be my brothers and sisters under the same God. I once smoked a cigarette rolled by a direct descendant of the Prophet Muhammad.

Maybe God has given us different paths to follow – that could also be the case, I don't know.

I chose not to become Jewish because I do not believe that God would exclude himself to 15 million people out of 7 billion without offering a chance of redemption. As a Christian, I believe that the coming of Christ superseded the Mosaic covenant – thus I do not feel bound to follow Rabbinical law, such as that of Leviticus or Deuteronomy, those parts of the bible which are often considered barbaric in contemporary times, such as the stoning of homosexuals or stoning women who have premarital sex. I believe that these applied only to one tribe, at one point in time, under conditions of extreme duress, prior to the redemption of mankind.

I did not choose to convert to Islam, because most western converts I see are motivated by sin.

If you are a Muslim reading this, take note of the motivations of those who seek to pursue your faith. Here is why: I know many who have converted solely for wealth, social connection, privilege, martial prowess, the promise of one of your women, or political favour. For instance, when I see Andrew Tate convert to Islam to be more like the Dagestani fighters he idealizes, I see him trading something which is eternal and transcendent for something that he can benefit from 'here and now.' I see him accrue things which only enable his wrath and pride. He may also find inner spiritual peace from this, but the intention of why one converts to a faith in the first place matters a great deal to me. Tate is not alone, I know several other westerners who converted to Islam because they believed they would become better warriors, fighters and businessmen. After Napoleon liberated Egypt, he nearly converted to Islam so that he could

46

lay claim to a powerful universal caliphate. Others still seem to be motivated by the promise of a submissive, unemancipated wife who is bound by religious law to obey the husband. It is much more difficult to keep a western woman happy, faithful and by one's side. This is the cost of free will. However, it is a cost I am willing to pay.

I find the sacrifice of freedom too great, and not necessary. The adherence to a universal moral law is different from deriving moral lessons from a universal model. The former does not account for relativities of culture, society or political system, while the latter allows for interpretation and relevant application in each context. I believe in the latter over the former because I believe human beings have free will for a reason, only under the conditions of freedom can we express real truth, and find true cultivation. Thus, I believe that one choosing to follow a moral path freely is more righteous than if one is forced to, even if only half of the people in a given land end up subscribing to said faith, rather than 99% of the people. I have heard too many of that faith say that 'we are supposed to sin,' because it is inherent in our nature, and not hold themselves to the idea that 'we should try not to sin.' Personally, I find it better that only half of everyone follows a faith, and does it properly, than if everyone were to do it, and lowers the standard of adherence for everyone. Yet this is endemic in the structures of both.

I do not consider all alcohol consumption to be necessarily sinful. I find it brings out the truth – if alcohol makes you sin, it was because sin was already in your heart. I believe in laying things out and confronting them. If you cannot drink without sinning, then by all means abstain from drinking, but I do not believe complete abstinence is necessary in all cases for a forthright moral life. If drinking causes you to forget or forsake your faith, it was not the alcohol which made you do so. Abstinence of this kind is often a mask, real truth is in liberation.

There is a riddle, whereby two angels in the afterlife are each stood by a door. One door goes to heaven the other to hell. There is no difference in appearance between either angel or either door. However, the one guarding the door to hell is a demon in disguise, while the other, guarding the door to heaven, is a real angel. The only difference between the two of them is that the angel will always tell the truth, and the demon will

47

always lie. You can ask them anything you like – how can you tell which is which?

In the Gospel, Jesus returns from a journey and says that Satan took him to a place of great height and promised him all the riches and kingdoms of the world. He denied himself these temptations and returned to us, to be sacrificed for our redemption.

In the [redacted], [redacted] returns from a journey and says that an Angel took him to a place of great height and promised him all the riches and kingdoms of the world. He accepted these things, and in a short amount of time he and his posterity conquered most of the known world and the seats of ancient empires – all of Arabia, Mesopotamia, Egypt, most of North Africa, Spain, and made significant inroads into France, only being stopped by a Christian Frankish King.

The answer to the riddle is: to ask both angels what the other angel would say about them.

On Sin

What if I told you *why* sin was bad?

Otherwise it wouldn't make sense why anyone would choose not to indulge themselves when they otherwise would. It seems perfectly rational to enjoy life as much as possible while we are here. In fact, without the consideration of anything *beyond* the world, the maximization of pleasure within it seems to be an ultimate value. This is what Epicurius believed, the father of Epicureanism, and was later championed by Jeremy Bentham, the father of Utilitarianism.

In both of these schools of thought, the goal is to maximize pleasure and minimize pain. But later forms of Epicureanism and Utilitarianism took on increasingly advanced forms, and the idea of *delayed gratification* was introduced. They noticed that it was often better to deny oneself pleasure in the present in exchange for more pleasure later on. If one introduces the notion of a 'grand design,' or 'ideal form of life' to the equation, the latter so being the case in John Stuart Mill's principle of Eudemonia, then the Abrahamic notion of 'sin' begins to make sense to our contemporary understanding.

'Sin' is originally an Aramaic word, which means to 'miss the mark.' As in, if someone is shooting an arrow, and it misses the target, it is a 'sin.' This is very telling. In the Christian tradition, we have some amount of free will, yes, but there is a higher intention for us if we can stay voluntarily, on the correct trajectory. When we 'sin,' therefore, we are choosing to divert from the trajectory for some other immediate gain.

I imagine sin as follows. God has shot you, like an arrow, towards a specific target. Every time you sin, you choose to deviate from the path He has shot you towards. As you fly over the battlefield, you are tempted to swing down and hit a foot soldier, maybe an officer or commander. Worse, a tree or just the ground. But God has aimed you straight at the heart of a general.

There are certain motivations that almost never yield the best possible outcome. These temptations are ever present, the more we do them, the more we divert from the best possible outcome. The world pressures us towards these motivations. Our biology and psychology are hard wired this way.

Some examples, the first ones off the top of my head:

Wrath: I knew a man who got hit by a car while riding a bicycle. He assaulted the driver and got a criminal record, when he otherwise could have gotten a 50 grand payout from the insurance.

Gluttony: I was once supposed to go out to the club with a mate, but he ate too much and got a belly ache and couldn't come. At the event, I ran into both my ex and his ex, who he was still in love with. I got with my ex, and his ex 'wing manned' by getting with another guy.

Envy: I used to despise a guy I went to school with because he was more athletic and charismatic than me, but was always nice to me. Rather than become his friend and see what I was doing wrong, I contented myself to dislike this person – on account of his positive traits of humility and discipline.

Lust: I once had a crush on a girl in my dorm, but her roommate was being flirty with me so I got with her instead. Thus, I blew my chances with the girl I really fancied.

Pride: I knew a guy who got shot because he couldn't handle being disrespected by a stranger at a house party. Had he not taken himself so seriously, he would not have gotten shot.

Sloth: I know someone who missed their big break in acting because they overslept and missed their shoot. They couldn't be bothered to come, and the replacement actor landed a major TV role from the connections they made while covering for him.

Greed: I recently brought a friend along to a dinner at a Greek restaurant, and he was unwilling to share his food in the traditional Greek communal style of eating. He also insisted on paying only for what he had, despite trying other people's food and having plenty of disposable income. He did not know that the other people there included the CEO of a tech company, the heir-apparent of a dukedom and an Olympic athlete, all of whom he would have benefited from befriending. He was seen as stingy and greedy, and was never invited around again.

I walk through life assuming that if I retain my moral composure and act forthrightly, then there is a trajectory that can be the best of all possible scenarios. I believe that it is my choice whether I follow it or not, whether there is anyone there to see it, or not. I assume moral responsibility and take accountability for my actions. That is the essence of free will, and it is the precondition for freedom.

If something goes wrong in my life, I ask myself: what sin did I commit to bring this about? How did my actions deviate my trajectory from what could have been? I 'take inventory,' assessing how my actions, my sins led to this outcome. I use these considerations to try and improve my moral character, and make myself more capable of handling freedom.

A Catholic priest once told me that God gives us free will in faith that humanity will ultimately choose light over darkness.

That is how I reconcile free will with fate.

On Christian Martyrdom

Luke 6:27-28

I do not believe it is for Christians to demean, oppress, or shame homosexual individuals. It is also not their place to restrict their behaviour or attempt to relegate them to the shadows. Rather I find the Christian doctrine instead inclines us to overcome our nature in this respect, approach them as individuals with care and understanding, seeing them rather as victims who have suffered – and must be protected. I do not believe Christians are bound to Israelite Laws such as Leviticus 20:13.

If one sees a man who is missing a nose, the initial reaction is probably a feeling of shock and uneasiness. One probably does not particularly enjoy seeing it, or thinking about it. However, only an evil and wicked person would be mad at that person for walking around with no nose. One does not accost him, or accuse him of cutting off his nose by choice. Yet, he might be proud of his face, for it represents the hardships he has overcome. It's a way to cope, to be proud of it. If you see a man missing a nose, you know that to be kind and respectful to him is the correct thing to do.

I do not believe that Christ would call us to be hateful towards a homosexual who acts out. In LGBTQ demonstrations, I believe that what they are really asking for is love, protection and understanding. From what I have been told by LGBTQ individuals, they feel that these are the things which they have lacked in life, which is the reason why they turn to mass movements.

If you see the emergence of these mass movements which agitate for their recognition in society, will hatred make their calls stronger or more diminished? Is your hatred coming from a place of wrath, seeking revenge for molestations of young men, pride, in one's moral high ground, or even envy that they engage in sin with impunity while you are bound by rules?

Homosexuality in society has been described by some as a disease. More accurate descriptions have described it as a symptom of a disease.

Let us imagine it is a symptom: Imagine a rash on an ill body. The rash is a symptom of chicken pox. Is the correct response to scratch it violently, and excise the inflamed skin? Or rather, is the correct response to be gentle, and apply a soothing ointment, protect the skin and leave it otherwise as undisturbed as possible? Even if your instinct tells you to scratch it, and you may think that getting the fluid out will solve the problem, a bit of wisdom and restraint will show you otherwise. There have always been people with homosexual tendencies in society. They only organize and take on political forms out of defence, in response to attack.

I have heard many conservatives describe that many homosexuals are the product of molestation – if you truly believe that to be the case, then how can you justify being hateful and cruel to one who has suffered this terrible fate?

Christ commanded us to love one another as he has loved us. He forgave adulterers.[7] By doing otherwise, you are only worsening the situation – forcing a pushback across the rest of society, where an ideology – which I agree is harmful – is only deeper entrenched as a reaction.

Sin begets sin, darkness cannot drive out darkness. Only light can do that[8].

---

[7] John 8:1-30,
[8] MLK

The Science of Sexual Relations

Free-Form Thoughts, handwritten in London and the Cotswolds, Summer of 2023

Not wanting to fuck it up fucks it up. How to detach, while remaining there?

Remain steady and unwavering.

Men and women different but compliment rather than compete. Masculine and Feminine polarity ordained in nature.

I don't believe in love, I believe in [redacted].

Men and Women equal before God, but Men given Force and Responsibility. A weaker vessel is not an inferior person, delicate yet not frail. Strength does not denote quality.

Man honours female beauty. Through chivalry man honours God.

Abstinent because I want to be sure. One more woman, for all my days.

Never falling short, never missing.

Men should be out doing man's work, not fussing about with the ladies.

Kardashians only go for [redacted] guys because they're the only ones who would never say no.

[redacted] should definitely become Catholic owing to his relationship with his mother.

Man thrives on anxiety. It needs him so much.

The tension of opposition, the reconciliation of opposites.

Many feel they are too ugly inside to be loved, but being loved is when healing happens.

"Your country has dysgenic breeding properties"

What's with this London lady-cop and her kinky pink handcuffs?

You're the girl of my dreams.

You're still dreaming. Wake up!

Handwritten on Muji 64 Page, Semi-Bleached.

During its early developmental years, modern Germany (Bundesrepublik Deutschland) was thoroughly fucked in every orifice by the allied powers. Now, to gain validation from the international community, it fucks itself.

German schools in Nordrein-Westphalia now have designated, supervised sexual experimentation rooms for pre-school age children. They believe that otherwise, they would do it in unsupervised settings, which would be more dangerous for the children. Many modern liberal families also have a very *laissez-faire* attitude to experimentation in the household. In both instances, the adults are trying to keep the children safe by at least relegating it to a safe and controlled environment. I believe that prepubescent sexual play should not be tolerated at all, and more attention should paid to them in their early years to prevent it. That is because those children will internalize later in life that they can only be validated by others through their willingness to do sexual acts.

In ancient and indigenous societies there were instances of transgenderism. Native Americans are one example. However I think we misinterpret this. I grew up around a lot of Mexicans[9], there was a phenomenon among the young Mexican boys, that they would form gangs of their own kind and find one 'runt of the litter' who they would bully and beat up, yet still have around. They would often make this one little, weaker Mexican kid suck their dicks and sometimes fuck him in the ass. Eventually, the Mexican girls would take pity on this one little male reject and bring him into their fold. They would protect him and the boys would stop fucking with the reject. They wanted to avoid being estranged from the females who they would later want to get with upon their quinceañeras.

This little runt of the litter would then be socialized as a female, and the distance from masculinity paired with the early same sex experiences would be conducive to homosexual thoughts. In addition, he would later

---

[9] I lived opposite Cadillac Drive in San Jose, California for four years.

internalize his prepubescent sexualization as the only means to attain validation from his peers, orienting him towards hypersexuality. Moreover, awe and admiration of women and their ability to wield power over the boys without the use of coercive force would lead him to place women upon a 'divine feminine' pedestal. This made him de-sexualize women, out of too much fear, respect and gratitude, and he would come to reject his own masculine impulses. His ideal form becomes a woman; not a man.

By the time of their adulthood they are a gay man, or transgender.

This is the origin of many people who have this identity. The memory of being removed from the gender binary by the force and sexual will of others.[10]

I knew a Hispanic trap in high school, they described a feeling of being akin to one of Skyrim's 'Dragon Priests,' devotees to the other side, having felt rejected by their own.

What then of the Aztecs, and the Incas? What manner of rampant sexual horror would they have unleased on their subjects? What manner of uninhibited freedom of the dark vestiges of the spirit were cultivated in the dark abysses of the jungles of South and Central America? What would they have done to the little boys, who lacked in strength and were unable to engage in warfare? What practice, what sport must they have made in their youth – practice for the reproduction of their kind in adulthood? How do their descendants, the savage Aztec warriors of today pass themselves on?

In any case I imagine something similar happens to a lesser extent in English and French boarding schools.

Look to Thailand today for an even more interesting insight on the phenomenon of transgenderism, a massive number of men pursue the extremely tough combat sport of Muay Thai, in which the masculine ideal is pushed to its absolute limit. Tongkat Ali and other testosterone

---

[10] Paglia, Holloubecq, anecdotes from people I have met

stimulating drugs and plants are taken to increase the androgenic element. At the same time, there is a pushback in the opposing corners of society, the men who are physically incapable or unwilling to meet this standard of masculinity become 'Ladyboys[11]' and whore themselves out to businessmen and western tourists. Ironically, drugs which increase testosterone like Tongkat Ali, also increases estrogen if the body cannot maintain the upkeep of testosterone production. This is because free radical testosterone binds with other hormones in the body to form phytoestrogens, which increase feminine properties, and changes one's neural chemistry. Thus, if the body cannot block the reuptake of testosterone into phytoestrogens, then the body and mind become effeminized by the abundance of estrogenic hormones.

Thus in places like Thailand, where the masculine ideal is pushed to it's greatest height, a long dark shadow is cast into the underworld.

All of this begins in youth, with the organization of masculine and feminine hierarchies. Under the conditions of normal human society, an excessive push towards the androcentric element bodies forth a reaction in the form of a parallel double movement towards feminization. This takes on sexual forms under the conditions of prepubescent sexual activity.

Additionally, sexually laissez-faire attitudes in childhood promote a double movement towards both hypersexuality and sexual repression. From readings on Weimar Germany, sexual psychology and from anecdotal observations on human nature in general, I believe that the sudden and intense sexual liberation of 1920's Weimar Germany was in part responsible for the political movements which surrounded the principle of 'sexual repression' in the 1930s. If this is the case, the emergence of the European far right from the mid-2010s can be in kind interpreted through a sexual lens, looking at the period of the 'Noughties,' or late 1990s in which sexual customs among the European pubic became liberalized. The change in sexual norms had the effect of relaxing advertisement regulations, fostered the widespread proliferation of

---

[11] Technical term

pornographic content, and liberalized sexual education, all of which had a constitutive effect on the youth of the early Gen-Z. This generation was uniquely hypersexualized at a very young age, and are now projected to be, at the same time, the most right-wing and the most LGBTQ generation of all recent contemporaries.

The ancient Greeks embodied all of these things I have mentioned but more extreme.

On Bruce Jenner
Transcribed and Paraphrased from Birth of Tragedy, Nietzsche.
Flight from London to Crete, August 2023

Life for many is suffering. It is akin to a bush of thorns. Yet there is a beauty which makes people continue the suffering. This beauty is akin to a rose, which emerges from thorn-laden branches.

The creation of this beaty is the greatest triumph over the darkness of the world. It allows us to find meaning in the suffering and contemplation of life. Yet the beauty is deceptive.

Nature uses this beauty to achieve its goals. We reach for the beauty, but grab onto something else, something terrible. The primordial oneness of eternal suffering and contradiction requires the most delightful illusion of aesthetic for its redemption.

By instinct, we believe something is justified by it's aesthetic – but the reality is inverse.

Handwritten on Muji 64 page, semi-bleached.

Can an aesthetic justify one's existence? Or must one's existence justify their aesthetic?

The show 'Keeping up with the Kardashians' is extremely based.

It's not about the Kardashians. It's actually about Bruce Jenner, a good, God-fearing Christian conservative Republican American man, an all-star Olympic athlete, who once out-ran every single black man on the planet. In this epic, he is trying his best to protect his family from the degenerate vices of Los Angeles. It is a tragedy, you already know how it ends.

It is a real-life drama of the spirit, telling the tale of this man trying to save his family from the dark atavistic forces of Los Angeles. At every turn, Rob Kardashian has his perverted friends over, being inappropriate with the young Jenner girls, corrupting them and making them do inappropriate things like dance half-naked on camera (episode 2 or something). Then, Kris takes the whole family to Mexico to do a sexy photoshoot, (episode 3 or something) and lies about it to Bruce, who rightfully objected to it and even flew out to catch them in the act. Even though he caught his spouse lying to him, he has no power to do anything. He is routinely emasculated in this way.

All of this degenerate shit and far worse is done behind Bruce's back, who tries everything in his power to protect his family. Yet his wife, and the dark, degenerating atavistic forces seethe their way into his family. He is powerless, and the powerful 'yin' energies saturate, dominate and overcome him and his family. He is rendered mere bull, powerless sperm donor to the primordial hive queen.

I only saw three or four episodes, but this is all I needed to understand the meta-narrative of the show. I enjoy looking at pop culture to understand broader trends of contemporary social phenomena. They would not make so much money off of this show, nor would it be so resonant unless it reflected a general trend which was prevalent across the social morass.

More importantly – it is important to see what the 'ideal' is shown to be for a great segment of society. When there is an ideal put forward that is associated with luxury, fame and power, people who see it will almost inevitably converge on that ideal, either consciously or subconsciously. I have asked normies around the world, in Ukraine, England and everywhere in between about this show, they say they like it because 'it is so glamorous,' or 'when I watch it, I like to pretend that it's my life.' In a sense, they seem to live vicariously through the Kardashians. This creates a void in their own life which beckons to be filled.

The image and aspiration of the Kardashian family itself provides the most delightful illusion for those who already bear the cost of suffering and contemplation in the world. Through the screen, an object of pure aesthetic representation, their lives become justified. Like a rose amongst a sea of thorns, the idea of a Los Angeles in a world of Birmingham's or Kiev's becomes the most powerful illusion which justifies the existence of those living in aesthetic and material misery. The attainment of this life, this aesthetic, this look, becomes a reason to continue living. Life is ugly for most, but the idea of it being someday beautiful makes it worth it to keep trying.

 I'm not even talking about the family's cosmetics, nor their marketing strategies when I say that for them, 'an aesthetic justifies one's existence.'

The primordial oneness associated with a domination of feminine energy can be seen in the homogenizing tendencies of the aesthetic ideal created by this family. When women of all different races and appearances emulate the characteristic Jenner/ Kardashian 'look,' ethnic differences seem to disappear.

This seems to be the hidden intention of nature herself – a force far more profound than the family's business interests and moneyed backers. The cash nexus itself, despite what you may think, is indeed a product of this dark feminine. It only uses the light and lesser masculine as it's means.

By eradicating the difference in appearance through converging on one apparent 'look,' a sexual egalitarianism is created for women. It becomes less possible for potential male suitors to distinguish particular characteristics and select for specimens of greater sexual, genetic and personal compatibility. Individualities are stripped away and we are incidentally made more akin to the world of the east, in which the vortex of biomass subsumes all within, and homogenizes.

In the world of this aesthetic, and for those captured by this dreamlike illusion, they are subjected to a real-world experiment in human biodiversity. The breakdown of natural differences, quirks and peculiarities lessen incompatibilities of taste in one respect, while incidentally maximizing the importance of one sole real factor: net worth and monetary value.

What could the value of a secure, virtuous and protecting family, that profound biological impulse of the higher man, have offered in exchange for such power and influence? What alternative could Bruce Jenner have offered, more valuable than to be the ideal around which the socio-sexual tastes of a whole world increasingly converge? Just that, individuation, rather, the masculine impulse to overcome gravity, and escape from the endless morass. Like a Saturn V rocket escaping the event horizon of a black hole, far from reaching for the rose and grabbing thorns, the path Bruce Jenner sought was to brave the bees, and get the honey.

Maybe Kris emasculated him so hard that he became a woman. Or maybe he was just so based that he realized the only way she could take down the system was from within. In the latter case, her existence, *what she does,* justifies her aesthetic, *how she looks*.

The people need an ideal to look to, and a caste to guide them to it. England is fortunate because they already have one. Rather they *still* have one.

Most societies on earth find a balance, but they tend towards certain directions.

The East can be conceived of as 5 men who want what the West has, and think they deserve it and that everyone in the west should die. There are also 5 women, who wear thick makeup, don't care about freedom and want to share in the booty.

The West can be conceived of as 9 LGBTQP, people of colour, Women, and disabled folx, who all say that the West doesn't deserve what they have, and that all straight white men should die. There is also one straight white man who wears all black and says his only purpose is to die.

Which side will win and who am I?

Russians do not tolerate outright homosexuality. Yet, male Russian society is extremely gay. I was once in Eastern Europe dancing and wrestling in a park with some dear friends drinking vodka and listening to Limp Bizkit late one night when an American tourist randomly came bumbling about asking for directions. Hearing her speak English I gave her directions and offered that she was welcome to join us and our Slavic soiree. With one Russian friend under each arm, dancing together, I asked her if she knew why there were no homosexuals in Russia. She said she didn't know. So I kissed both my mates on the cheek and said 'because Russian men are already so fucking gay!"

The idea is, that in order to participate in the masculine hierarchy, you cannot have ulterior or sus motives that are sexual or morally corrupt in nature. To be part of the team, this sacred bond, you can't be there for some gay shit. You have to be focused on the mission, the higher ideals, the faculties, the objectives of the group. The boys cannot be worrying about you making advances on them, worry about you just being there to 'get some.' And when there are no 'foxxes in the henhouse,' so to speak, it allows for a very silly, very affectionate, 'fake gay' playful attitude between men to emerge. This is natural and sacred, to defile this is to violate the most precious thing which the Russians have. They do not have the same decadent luxuries which we enjoy in the west, nor a society which is conducive to the flowering of one's individuality. Rather, the bond between their fellow man, this fraternity is what gives their life meaning and justification. This is the foundation of their whole society, and for this sacred bond, Russian men are willing to die.

Thus, the way it appears to the westerner, who looks in and observes is, everyone gets to be a little gay. If I was to explain it to a western homosexual I would say: think of toddlers getting a cookie in day care, but only one, they are told: 'you get what you get and you don't throw a fit.' If you're not satisfied by this playful little boy-like affection, if you're not grateful for what you're already getting, then the rest of the gang will beat you up and exclude you, with great vengeance; for you have soiled and made dirty and profane something sacred. They know how atomized and cold the west is, with its lack of deep social bonds, the conditionality of social relations, they know in their blood that their very survival depends on the tightness of the group. If you reveal yourself to have ulterior motives, corrupting this sacred bond of transcendental importance for mere sexual gratification, low and fleshy desires, it would be just as bad as if you were there to rob them, or take advantage of them monetarily – you're just a cruiser, a grifter.

In any case many Russians probably do have gay thoughts, that isn't the problem so much as living it out and giving into these impulses. If you give into these impulses, which produce no children nor have any biological utility, it indicates to them that you lack the ability to control impulse – you just let horniness control you and thus you cannot be trusted to be there for motives above sexual cravings. American football teams and Canadian hockey teams also have this playful fake-gay brotherly spirit but they are usually also infested with actual [redacted].

Think of it like this: White Western Women will go to the gay club so that they can dance with their friends to 80s disco music without having to worry about horny men who are just there to try and fuck them. Likewise, Russian men have organized their society so that they can dance with their friends to 80s disco music without having to worry about horny men who are just there to try and fuck them.

In White/ middle/ Conservative America, the problem is that masculinity has become too inclusive. Bullying was outlawed after Columbine in 1999, and rigid rules on sexual advance and flirting which sterilized all forms of courtship were implemented after Woodstock '99 of the same year. These two events completely ended the hypermasculine culture of American High Schools cultivated by the CIA during the Cold War that Europeans might have seen or been aware of from films like Porky's or American Pie. It should be noted that in doing so they scrubbed clean the worst degenerate vices of this culture, though it should also be noted that these are very quickly coming back in darker and more atavistic forms.

Amongst the more conservative strata of America, in the hopes of avoiding anyone becoming gay or a school shooter, bullying itself is outlawed, especially among Whites, to ensure that nobody falls victim to the 'runt of the litter' mentality present among the Mexicans and Blacks. No one is bullied out of 'being a man,' so that in theory, fewer people become gay (or a school shooter). But then there is less of a standard to hold everyone else to, 'being a man' comes to mean more things, so it also means less things, and the entire masculine hierarchy backslides.

Essentially, while there is more homophobia in Russia, the backsliding in America is not in terms of gay behaviour, but in masculine virtue itself. It is coupled with the drive towards being a good businessperson rather than a man first and foremost, with less masculine pressure placed on the individual. Instead, being a strong economic unit is the primary objective of the American socialization system. Russia, as I will describe, does not have this problem.

This loss of masculinity in western society has to then be compensated for by women, which creates a whole plethora of social problems and relational issues, with them having to take up the mantle of leading the couple, which is very unsexy and unpleasant for them despite how much they say it's fine. They even had to invent a whole new wave of Feminism to gaslight themselves into thinking it's somehow okay. It's not. It all results from western man's laziness to hold himself to a proper standard, in which his masculine nature can flourish. Under this condition, western women's femininity would also be allowed to flourish, and balance and harmony between the sexes could be re-cultivated. However, this would entail western man having to deal with the worst excesses of his masculine impulses, either through religion and its sacrifices, or a moral code and its self-discipline.

Though many people would rather have fun and enjoy the hedonistic pleasures associated with Godlessness and consumerism, becoming weak and letting someone else bear his burden, rather than bearing the cost of maintaining the bulwark against his masculinity's worst excesses. Then, out of his own inability or strength to express raw and unpasteurized masculinity, he just lets himself descend into weakness and femininity, where there is less of a path of opposition. This is most evident in the workplace, where the levelling effects of the office and the temptations of pride and greed thwart the spirit of independence and self-overcoming present in healthy men.

This is a paradox, because even though the masculine hierarchy has backslid in the West and America there are still more gays in the West than in the East and Russia. Why is this?

Imagine a comet flying in the cosmos, but all you see is it's wake. If you were to walk through a modern western university, it is unlikely that you would assume that this university would field great Olympic athletes of tremendous strength and vigour. You would likely rather be unimpressed, and if you were of any amount of vitality, you would reckon yourself among the elite superstratum of the physical specimens there on campus.

But that is only because you don't see the rugby, hockey, or American football team, who remain locked away and jealously guarded, nor those on the fringes who self-cultivate in the abstract. You don't see the titans of sublimation that only the individualism of the west can cultivate. Russia has athletes as well, some even akin to those of the west, but rarely do you see the coinciding of near-unlimited potential paired with the means and method to reach their full expression like you do in the west. There are enough for the Olympics and the upper echelons of international sport, and regional competitors are strong. Less often do they also study finance or the sciences at the highest level which cultivates the mind to a similar or exceeding degree. A Russian athlete is usually an athlete first and foremost, while the American reaches and exceeds the same level for fun, for vanity, to create a physical foundation upon which they strive for some real, greater purpose. Gerald Ford or Arnold Schwarzenegger, for instance.

When you walk around the streets of America, Canada or England, you don't see those men, whose families themselves uphold capitalism, with all of its backsliding and emasculating pressures, to preserve their own existence. You don't see the monsters of will, beacons of hereditary nature, who lie in wait, and cultivate the conditions for their own survival.

If you don't see them, these gators deep in the swamp, then many things about the West don't make sense.

You wouldn't understand, for instance why so many women hate men. Often, it is because they accidentally relegated themselves to cannon fodder for these beasts of will who would never have the intention of committing to them exclusively. That is also why polyamorous relationships are becoming more common in the west, the higher types set the trend and everyone else expects the same. You wouldn't understand why there are so many emasculated men, until you understand who broke their will at an early age, until you understand what they were up against. You wouldn't understand why the west rejects the 'mob,' until you understood the degree to which it thwarts the potential of the few. Someone from the east would never understand the degree of freedom needed to reach this terrible, titanic height of greatness, if it were not for the deep recesses of [redacted] to which one is equally free to fall.

Beyond the university, which I speak of as a metaphor, I refer specifically to the special forces apparatuses of the west, and certain aspects of the military more generally.

I was in Greece recently, and if I was an alien, I would be puzzled as to why all of the tall and athletic men, the heirs of the ancient Greeks, are locked away in a fortress, jealously guarded by the state, while all the beautiful women locked outside are left to ravenously compete for the scraps and leftovers.

The truth is, the state is saving the good men for the transcendent. They are saving them, for Turkey.

The special forces apparatuses of the US, Britain and France, as well as other NATO countries are the same way. They have skimmed the cream from the top of their societies and churned them into butter. The butter sinks to the bottom, and displaces the milk. The eastern countries look to the jar and say, 'look, they are all milk, and so much of it!'

They, much like the libertarian right in America, fail to recognize that once one drains the swamp, they must contend with the gators. And neither you nor them have any idea how deep that swamp goes.

What you see is a society which makes no sense, which suffers from the consequence of an invisible abundance of strength. Walk down the street and you will find that there are none to maintain this strength, none who carry the mass which displaces the fluid. The truly individuated and self-actualized who justify all of it, these Olympians who continually recreate and redeem the entire system, whose existence justifies the aesthetic, you will not find them amongst the many. They are busy defying gravity.

The eastern critics see the wake, but not the comet. They see not cause, but consequence.

Russia does not have the same capitalistic impulses as the west. For all of this society's faults, they are still oriented towards the Soviet ideal of cultivating the full human potential. There is far less drive to cultivate the masses as individuated, atomized economic units. Rather, the objective is the cultivation of an entire people as a supreme social and political unit. The latter is especially the case for the past 15 years, with the creation of a Russian 'civic nationalism,' to ward of an unchecked extreme far right. Incidentally, far right cells in Russia are one of the only indigenous and organic forms of civil society that have ever emerged without foreign support in that country.

The pasteurization and integration of these tendencies into the mainstream has been a hallmark of Russian social policy, especially since 2012, which in part explains the Russian government's hardline stance on homosexuality – it constitutes an overlap between the religious conservative lobby and the relatively 'pagan' ultranationalist movements, which dissident Alexei Navalny was once aligned with.

This policy has been relatively effective at creating a quite healthy and politically inclusive Russian society, Putin enjoys *real* popular support, and a lot of it. Rather than cultivating the individual, the object is to cultivate the whole society and the social bonds which mediate social relations. A communal, collective approach is favoured over western individualism. However, I do not believe that is the only reason why there are less homosexuals in Russia.

Aside from the less intense capitalistic impulses towards atomization, which create distance between males allowing for an eros, or 'sexualized distance,' to form, paired with primal limitation, subjection of the will and the release of sexual or other forms of repression and sublimation, which I will discuss in 'on cocaine,' Russia also did not have the same pushback against unchecked masculinity at the turn of the century, they didn't have Columbine or Woodstock '99 – and they chose to bear the ills and consequences of what they had through political, not social repression.

Political repression from the top down incidentally had the effect of strengthening Russian social bonds from the bottom up, which did not create the social conditions of individuality which allow for the full expression of homosexual tendencies, unlike in the United States where extreme individuality was forced on everyone from the bottom up around the turn of the new millennia.

However, since the assassination of Maxim Tesak in 2020, it seems the Russian government has made it clear that it is better to be gay than political opposition.

This creates an odd phenomenon, which is far more common among the European periphery than you might think, whereby Nazis are finding a home amongst the LGBTQ movement, finding more in common with them than with the main-line conservative strata which hunts them down. I have seen with my own eyes real neo-Nazis defend women and gays from the attacks of hateful East European men, who would say that gays and Nazis are their worst enemies. Gays generally don't care if someone is extremely right wing as long as they aren't necessarily homophobic, and Nazis generally don't care if someone is gay as long as they aren't a paedophile - it's usually cucks who take issue with people's fringe political views, and even then, it's usually because men who aren't afraid to express their dangerous opinions are the ones who are fucking all the women.

It actually makes a lot of sense, both gays and Nazis study art and philosophy, listen to Tame Impala and Rammstein, they are generally well-read, educated and smoke weed.

They also dress exactly the same.

There is an unchecked hypermasculine substratum aside from this in Russia, yes, but they are generally all heathens, criminals, gangsters and agents of oligarchs. The only place where this is not really the case is Chechnya, where the 'securitocracy[12]' is both devout Muslim and aligned with the security state. However, this is probably the exception which proves the rule, as nowhere else on earth is homosexuality more intensely forbidden.

But sexual chauvinism of all kinds is forbidden in Chechnya, not just homosexuality. A dear friend of mine was in Grozny, he got stabbed for wearing shorts and drinking a beer. While drinking beer was probably the main reason, he told me that he saw other people drinking beer and they were fine, so it was probably to do with wearing shorts in public, which was against the rules they have of modesty in appearance and self-exposure for men as well as women.

I ask you - why would Chechnya need this degree of sexual sterility?

---

[12] Richard Sakwa

In conservative parts of America, religion plays a similar function. Where Christianity is strongest, such as in the south, masculinity is most allowed to flourish. That is because the Christian doctrine serves as a bulwark against the worst and most destructive excesses of what men are capable of. It keeps in check man's wrath and lust, giving him sexual discipline and controlling his violent nature, while still preserving his vital energy and willpower. The ancient Greeks adopted Christianity so quickly and easily because it served to counter the problems that emerged from the excesses of their individual strength.

The problem is, that for some odd reason, American free-market capitalism and Christianity are often very closely allied. This doesn't make so much sense to me, as the former has a structural reliance on greed, pride and envy which is rather antithetical to the latter. Moreover, free-market capitalism can only thrive when the subject population has been subjected to intense primal limitation. When this has happened, the need for Christianity is far less obvious, because the natural, healthy primal will which needed to be reined-in in the first place is cut down. People with a thwarted will and curtailed strength then have no idea why they would ever need Christianity in the first place. A cat with no claws needs no clipping.

Interestingly, much of Eastern Europe is actually very non-religious, despite what they may like to pretend. The degeneracy is pushed underground, while those who have an impulse to individualism often leave to the west, so the lack of and need for moral standards is not seen. In any case, when I moved to Eastern Europe I found myself free for the first time from the limiting pressures that had been endemic and all-encompassing in the United States.

Though now, I see Manchester would have sufficed.

From Notes

(Free market capitalism) creates creates cucks and cuckers, rich fucks and cock suckers.

I would rather live in a society of gays than a society of cucks.

73

That is because a cuck is just a cucker in waiting – while a gay has accepted his fate.

.

On Cocaine

Indulgence negates the ultimate effect. Excesses reveal the ultimate truth.

Too much satisfaction breeds satiation. Let the means be of an end.

Caught in a daze, down in a spiral, wondrous explosion; miasma of colours, dizzying hues of all tones and shades, a marvellous spectrum in which all is conceivable.

Crazy, deluded, schizoid imagining of things and superimposing a mysticism onto that which is real, turning truth into falsehood.

Now is not the time to feel guilty. Save that for your wife and children. Enjoy now the imminence.

I put the 'Ken' in 'Kensington.'

Do not call yourself [redacted] then shirk the excesses before you. The real truth is found in Titanic excesses, independent objectivity comes with a cost, but who knew it was not for you to pay?

I am a neoclassicist, not a classist.

Embrace the good too with equanimity. How do the sheikhs of Arabia justify their wealth, their excesses and consumption? Complete and utter detachment (it's all a piss take)

Real faith is to show what is within.

Unholster your thoughts, enter the sacred temple.

Rishi Sunak is my favourite Taurus.

Live a life which justifies its excesses. Then, one comes into excess – and exceeds.

This is your down time, your moment of rest. Recognize that you are on the path of ascent, this is fleeting. You have reason in any case, for your *emptiness.* Have some zinc and put on a happy face.

Things never get easier – but you will get stronger.

Remain steady and unwavering, and ride the tiger.

Handwritten on Muji unbleached, 64 page.

If you're a man, Cocaine makes you gay. Or a sexual predator. It depends whether you sniff it with men or women. If you are a woman, cocaine turns you into a ravenous [redacted] and makes you cheat on your man.

This is because chemically, your brain can't tell the difference between sniffing coke and rubbing one out. It's the same chemicals being released. If you're sat around a bunch of mates, and your brain thinks you're having a wank, you're going to subconsciously associate sexual gratification with being around the boys. If you're a girl, sat around 10 guys in a living room, and your brain thinks you're spanking the monkey, what's the next step up from there in the mind's eye? If you're a man in the former case, over a long enough time frame, the subconscious mind will get confused, and your increasing number of homosexual thoughts will confuse you into thinking you might be a [redacted].

If you're a man, sniffing coke with girls, you will subconsciously internalize that it is okay to 'gratify yourself' in their presence, and you will become far too comfortable making sexual advances. If your subconscious thinks that it's all right to masturbate together, it is much less of a leap for your mind to say, 'might as well have a shag,' and to assume that it is a given. It is well known that people who masturbate a lot have a hard time controlling themselves sexually around women, and are more likely to be creepy, perverted or pushy towards women. And vice versa. Search your memory and you will know that what I say is true.

Some people, who sniff coke with both men and women can sort of walk the line, flirting with both the aesthetic of being gay and a sexual predator, while probably not actually being either. Think of the aesthetic of David Bowie, but I think he probably sniffed a lot less coke than you might imagine. Perhaps I'm biased. I love David Bowie.

What makes it worse is that it's incredibly easy to fuck a girl if you're both sniffing coke. Cocaine makes women horny, and if it's your coke, there is a clear power dynamic which is very arousing for them. Don't give me some nonsense about coke-dick, this only affects men with low testosterone. If your girlfriend has gone off to sniff some random guy's coke, *she's probably sniffing it off his cock.*[13]

---

[13] A number of people have said these exact words to me

Cocaine also makes *delayed gratification* nearly impossible. If you're running on racehorse Charlie, the dopamine flooding your brain makes it very difficult to wait. Even a pizza taking thirty minutes feels like two hours if you're hungry. Thus, if you're horny and on coke and around a lot of women, you will be a lot more pushy to try and get some ass. If you are a woman, you're more likely to let him hit that then and there than you normally think you would otherwise. Even if you have a man – eh, why not, what's the point? He won't know.

And vice versa, in both cases.

Pounding your brain with instant gratification makes it harder to be patient with things. Commitment and loyalty, among our greatest virtues, are made possible when we can resist impatience and anxieties long enough. You get what you give with most things in life, and I think relationships are this way as well. When it's hard to give, or takes time, or there are other obstacles you have, few among us have the self-discipline to maintain passion in the heart, that makes us give freely and with love. To keep the candle lit, great strain is required.

Why keep the candle lit, while you still have a few matches? Surely the next candle-fire will burn brighter, and flicker higher? Why shield myself in the face of a gust of wind?

For women as well, when you sniff coke, you are re-wiring your brain towards instant gratification. Relationships take time to build, working through things is difficult and not fun or sexy, and requires you to have patience. It requires you saying no to other possibilities. When you sniff coke, even on occasion, you make it nearly impossible for your brain to have that sort of patience. You re-wire your neural chemistry to be impatient, so that you will be more likely to leave for the next best thing as soon as it comes along.

If you're a guy sniffing coke with your other mates, and its just you guys, and there's no girls coming, and it's late and you want to party, well, let's just say that idle hands do the devil's work.

I had some friends in high school, many of them of high and noble spirit. My high school had the unfortunate practice of 'bussing,' where kids from the most violent ghettos in the city were transported by the busload across town and let loose on rich White and Asian kids in their local schools and neighbourhoods. Think of the H.G. Wells novel: 'The Time Machine,' with the Morlochs preying on the naïve, silly little Eloi. The least malevolent effect of this practice was that my friends had unlimited access to cocaine and other hard drugs. With trust funds and allowances from well-meaning parents, and a liberal education that stressed 'safe drug use,' rather than 'no drug use,' the local kids, including my friends would be sat in their cars until the early hours of the morning, sniffing away. At school, they would sniff coke off the bathroom pass and then hand it right back to the teacher.

I never really enjoyed it, it just made me anxious. I also grew up around addiction, so I quickly realized that I wanted nothing to do with it. I hated seeing my friends fiend over it. I especially hated seeing girls on it, how they would act all slutty around my friends to try and get free coke. They would take off pieces of clothing, and snuggle against them. Sometimes they would put their heads on my friends' lap, or touch their willies through their pants. Fortunately, my friends were usually too autistic to do anything with them, or were just too gay by that point. Usually, that is.

I always pitied these girls' boyfriends, who had no idea what they were getting up to with my buddies. The girls would laugh, and say 'oh, he thinks I'm having dinner with my family,' or 'I told him my grandmother is in the hospital, and I have to be with her.' Even to this day, seeing what I saw, having heard what I heard, I don't think I could ever be with a Californian girl again – I've just got the ick.

Really, I thought cocaine was a ridiculous waste of money – I had other expensive hobbies, dirt biking, mountain biking, cinematography, who could justify spending hundreds in a night just to sit in your homie's minivan until 3 AM? You're not gaining anything at the end of the day. Plus it was fucking nasty, the noise of it, the snorting, sharing the bill, the bloody noses and snot.

I left the group and started hanging out with other people. Another guy, Dickless Pete, also left for the same reason. Fast forward a year, and everyone who had stayed in that group, sniffing coke every other day, was on some gay shit, or worse, some predatory shit.

Rumours spread about them sucking each other off, together as a group, while this one Mexican guy did gay shit in jail, supposedly to get drugs. Another Mexican guy, who I never got on with, even got done for paedophilia. He went to jail after giving a 16 year old loads of coke and then banging her. That's because, like I said, Cocaine kills your ability to practice delayed gratification and wait. In this case, he could not wait two more years for her to be legal.

Another guy, an Indian fella who's dad worked for Google sent me loads of messages confessing his homosexual thoughts towards me while he was having a drug-induced psychotic break, though he hadn't been gay at all before. There was a Scandinavian exchange student, who had been a sick honkey and a world-class athlete, but he was also sniffing coke with these yutes. Years later, I saw him completely by chance in the street in a northern European city – and he was fruity as a Swedish fish. My best friend in the group, who is from a very famous American industrial family, got kicked out of the military for being on some gay shit. Just kidding – he got kicked out for coke, but he was also on some gay shit. One by one, everyone in the group had become gay as fuck, while Dickless Pete and I were the only straight ones left.

See American Psycho, what does Bateman say about 'the Yale thing?' 'He did a lot of cocaine and was probably a homosexual.' See it yourself. Next time you see a straight man on coke, or a gay man, ask yourself what the effect of cocaine is on one's sexuality.

It pumps the brain full of dopamine, and makes you dependent on a constant supply in order to function. The only other way to get that instant dump of dopamine is to beat your meat. So, the person who is doing loads of coke is up late at night, with all of their male friends, sitting in a little circle, pumping their brains full of dopamine, then going home, and frantically pumping their little willies to trigger the same exact chemical reaction in the brain. This is automatically going to rewire your neural circuity to associate these two behaviours, and soon, invariably, hanging out with your mates and banging coke will trigger the same triggers – making you horny!

If you're deprived, fiending, and out of coke, and its four AM, and you're horny as fuck, and you urgently need some dopamine in your brain, some instant gratification and catharsis, and it's just you and your mate, and you're out of coke, and the cost of getting a blowjob is that you have to suck him off as well, any hedonic calculation of what will yield the most pleasure relative to discomfort says that the choice of what to do here is obvious:

Don't fucking sniff coke!!!

In conclusion, a man who sniffs coke with his mates will become gay. A woman who sniffs coke will cheat on her man. A man sniffs a lot of coke with women will become a sexual predator. I don't need to provide evidence, the reasons I gave are good enough – like I said, search your memory and you will know that what I say is true. Thus, fellas, don't get with a girl if she's sniffing coke. We have to boycott the product and sanction the bad behaviour. And ladies, don't get with a fella if he sniffs coke, unless you're into pegging!

Just remember that jacking off and sniffing coke trigger the same brain responses. You wouldn't jack off in a circle of your friends unless you were gay. And you wouldn't jack off in the club unless you were a cuck in KitKat.[14]

For the record MDMA is just as bad. Being with a person can only ever make you feel so much love – there's only so much love you can actually feel at any one moment naturally. Else it just becomes meaningless and burnt out, and becomes something we reject. Pinging, getting that serotonin dump, how can a partner, who only has themselves as an abstract offering, compete with this feeling? For 10 quid, you can feel a deeper love than you will get from your partner. So why make the sacrifice of a lifetime of commitment to get something you could get so

_____

[14] The fourth best sex club in Berlin

much more easily and without the effort? Without the lifetime of commitment and sacrifice and work, just to feel a certain feeling and lift a certain existential burden, the need to feel loved? With only a pill, a 10 quid Tesla from Amsterdam, it is possible to feel this without the cost or consequence.

If I was an alien, come down from space to observe humanity, I would come to think that when the young generation flocks to a series of festivals, taking these pills to feel all these feelings at once, they are getting them out of the way before a lifetime of meaningless work. I would think that they are vaccinating themselves, against love.

Imagine you're a girl and you go to a festival with all your best friends. You take a bunch of MDMA, and have the most beautiful time of your life. You feel so much love, and you learn so much about yourself. You realize that what you thought you wanted isn't what you really want. You realize that you don't really love your boyfriend, and that you would rather be free and express yourself and get to know yourself and see what's out there in the big wide world, rather than be bogged down and stuck with just one person. You realize that life is about joy and experience, it's too short for 'meaningful sacrifice,' you want to see new people, taste all the flavours of life, that ultimately you are your own person and the executor of your destiny in this crazy journey called life. You're left thinking, 'what a beautiful world.'

Now imagine you're a guy, and the girl you had planned to marry goes to a festival and smashes loads of drugs with all her friends for a whole weekend. Then she randomly leaves you a few days later, because she decided she just wants to go and fuck a bunch of random guys. You're left thinking 'what the fuck?'

Return to the analogy of the alien, who has observed humanity at a distance, say for ten thousand years. They observe one person, one person who takes MDMA, a very, very recent invention that we have no idea of the long terms effects of, and that person decides that they no longer want to have children or build a family, and prefer their independence and to get to know themselves and live life to the fullest. How puzzling would it be for the alien, who observes this person take a pill, and then as a result chooses to end 4 billion years of continued evolution?

My point is, under no circumstances should you get with someone romantically if they are using any kind of hard drugs. Though I knew these lessons from childhood, I wasn't content to learn and internalize the lessons. I had to learn them twice, three times, because I let myself be gaslit into thinking that the first time was a fluke. Hard drug use, innocent as it may have seemed in the early 2000's, cost my family a broken home, and my father $80,000 in debt on credit cards that were under his name.

If you're reading this, and the truth of what I am saying is just now dawning on you now, then do what you have to do and fucking leave them! If they love you, and want to get back with you, let them get clean. Then it's up to you whether you want to take them back in the future and trust that their habits are relegated to the past, or not. Whatever you do, stick to your guns. You say you like a strong man or woman – fair enough, so do I. Test their strength, if a strong man puts pressure on a weak woman, she will run to a weak man for validation. Vice versa. If they do run to a weaker partner who won't put pressure on them, good, they have gone down and found someone in their own league.

If they actually love you, and aren't just using you, they will get clean and come back to you. If they don't, good f*cking riddance!

On Promiscuity later in life

When a man fucks many women, he gets validation for his insecurities and gratification for his penis. But women, more than men, release bonding hormones towards every new sexual partner. Because of this unequal trade, women who get fucked then forgotten about usually start resenting men.

When a woman gets fucked and then forgotten about a lot, she usually starts to hate men in general. Often times, this takes on a political form, and she becomes a feminist, sometimes a radical one. In doing so, she seeks to cut off sexual access towards men. This is perfectly rational – it could be a means to solve the social problem if done for the right reason. Heartbroken men often do the same thing – they cut off sexual access towards women by becoming a based sigma male, ie, a gentlemen. See any Jane Austen novel.

Another effect is that each time a man or woman gets seduced, fucked, then forgotten about, the amount of bonding-hormones either party is capable of releasing is decreased. A person who has had more than 20 sexual partners has a much more difficult time falling in love than someone who has had 2. The pairing of resentment against the opposite sex, paired with decreased ability to neurochemically bond leads to less people who want families, and more people who are willing to cheat on or divorce their future partners. That is why the divorce lawsuit industry has exploded since 1960. Moreover, it contributes to the demographic crisis which faces modern western nations, as it means less people are having children, due to both less marriages and more divorces when they do.

Both parties get short term enjoyment and validation. Pride and other things are stroked. Is it worth the resulting resentment, and the negative long term consequences across the whole of society?

It is well established in the scientific literature that the number of sexual partners prior to marriage drastically increases divorce rates. Studies generally find that with no previous partners, there is a 5% likelihood of divorce after 5 years. With ten or more previous sexual partners, the likelihood increases to about 35%-40%. Some studies put this figure up to 80%. This contributes to less children being born in general, and more divorces later on, which causes trauma to the children these couples do have. Children whose parents separate are shown to have greater difficulty forming stable bonds later in life, making it more difficult for them to start families as well. In more extreme cases, childhood traumas resulting from family difficulties have been shown to increase the likelihood of ADHD and delinquent behaviour, limiting success later in life.

I do not believe that one partner being 'bored' of their spouse justifies cheating, or an ensuing divorce. The sexual pleasure that one partner might get from sex with someone else get does not outweigh the pain and suffering of their spouse, or the children who see their family torn apart. If they did not want to be bored during marriage, they should not have slept around beforehand. Of course they will be bored with the same person for the rest of their life, but that is the cost of a stable union. If one chooses to get married, they should do so aware that it is a sacrifice of present enjoyment for the promise of a greater joy later on.

Heroin users complain that other activities no longer satisfy them. Clearly then they shouldn't use heroin. But when someone complains that monogamy doesn't satisfy them because they are used to fucking several different people, they get all touchy at the suggestion that they should have perhaps exercised more sexual discipline, and been less promiscuous. Is a short-term hookup worth the permanent effect on the brain's ability to form stable bonds? Are you exempt from considering this when you are drunk, horny or on holiday?

I should clarify that it is not only women who are victims of other people fucking them and then forgetting about them. Many men fall in love with women who have been with many partners, for whom it is very easy to walk away and move onto the next man. This leaves the man reeling in confusion and heartbreak, this is the target demographic of the likes of Andrew Tate and others.

But what causes a man to fuck many women? It's very clear – insecurity or horniness, or some combination of the two. Yet sleeping with many women causes great social ills, hyper promiscuity, as I have explained, leads to less people having children and an increased likelihood of broken families later in life – which again, creates childhood traumas for children who have been produced out of that union. Thus by any calculation, it yields more harm than good for men to run around fucking loads of women indiscriminately, and vice versa.

It is perfectly rational to seek the maximization of pleasure and minimization of pain. As I have described, this school of thought is called Epicureanism, and constitutes one of the most enduring schools of Classical Greek philosophy. The most advanced form of this is delayed gratification. This manifests in sexual relations through the construct of marriage, waiting until there is a positive commitment, a bond which is established based on the certainty that both parties are in fact, bound to one another and are capable of sustaining a relationship. One can choose to sacrifice all of the fleeting pleasures that will come from years of hookups in exchange for the joy of a committed marriage, and it will be worth it.

The Ancient Greeks looked up to promiscuous gods who themselves practiced infidelity. This validated their own infidelity. Is it any wonder that this society reeled from the consequences, and fell victim to demographic crisis itself?

A man who seeks sexual conquest for its own sake is either ignorant to the broader social effects he is creating, or is malevolent enough in spirit that he doesn't care, only seeking his own short-term gratification at much greater expense, to be paid by his future self and society as a whole. In most cases, he probably just can't control himself. And vice versa for women.

A man who sleeps around indiscriminately should be shamed. The more women he bangs, the more radical feminists he creates. The more men a woman bangs, the more Andrew Tate listeners she creates. Who could blame either party? Women rarely just want to be fucked and forgotten about, even if they gaslight themselves into thinking they do, under some kind of 'girl-boss,' don't-need-no-man mentality. Never does a man want a woman with 'experience' – how can he compete with the memories of 50 other guys? Who would want to? In both cases, heartbreak awaits. Both parties will find it harder to be vulnerable or find deep and meaningful connection with each other – I do not believe that it is wise to be promiscuous later in life, and these have been the reasons why.

A *fuckboy* who has ran through scores of women indiscriminately does not deserve a woman who has remained pure. He deserves a *slut.*

And vice versa.

The Science of Freedom

I understand how what I have written thus far might sound judgemental. If you feel judged, guilty, or made ashamed, or otherwise feel like this book constitutes a personal attack, let's address that.

When a vegan tells me I am evil for eating meat, I am do not feel ashamed. That is because I know that it is not evil to eat meat. However, when someone tells me I shouldn't hook up with random women, I do feel ashamed. That is because I already know, deep down, that I shouldn't be doing that.

So when I tell you that you would be wise to not be sexually promiscuous or use hard drugs, does it bother you? If it does, why is that?

If it bothers you because you already know it's true, and just don't like to hear it articulated, then let's look into why. It could be because you live in an 'ignorance is bliss' mentality, and would rather not know of the consequences of your actions, which is neither wise nor legitimate. Another reason could be because you demand validation for your bad behaviour, and thus seek to encourage others to follow in your footsteps. It makes it easier to bad things if you're not alone in doing them. In many cases, indulging in vices may constitute one's identity, so suggesting the idea that indulging in vices may be unwise feels like a personal attack.

That does not change the fact that it is unwise to sniff coke and sleep with everyone you meet. If you don't want to feel judged, don't read my book or don't be a [redacted].

Are you mad that the rest of the world is free to not celebrate and champion you? Are you mad that I don't follow you, that you're not the boss of me? Or do you just want others to make your mistakes, so you can feel validated in your bad decisions?

If you choose to make mistakes, at least don't pull down others with you.

That is where the question of freedom enters the picture.

People are free to make their own decisions. However, the cost of this freedom is that they must be able to handle the consequences of their freedom. When people cannot handle the consequences of their freedom, they put the costs onto others, and then invariably, they lose their freedom. This happens on both the individual level and the national level. A country which is a pariah state, and engages in wanton aggression usually does not say sovereign for long. The same goes for individuals, usually they soon find themselves in jail or worse. Not in all cases, though – only when truly un-justified.

In the case of promiscuity, people often say that they express their own freedom and liberation in the form of sexual expression. However, I offer the case that far from being free, promiscuous people sleep around because they are dependent – slaves to the demands of their lower organs and their insecurities which demand validation from others. Likewise, a nation which invades others is often either a slave to it's military industrial organs, or is masking its own insecurities, be they energy, strategic, or political.

The more partners one has before marriage, the more likely they are to get divorced or become abusive. Likewise, the more diverse the makeup of a country, the more likely the country is to either fall apart or become tyrannical. Look to the cases of Charles still being in love with Camilla, and the Sudanese government still being in love with Sharia law. In each case, Diana Spencer and Christian South Sudan both defected, got with other people and ruined the other's reputation. Universal phenomenon echo each other at different cosmological levels.

One should be glad rather than mad when one's bubble of ignorance is popped. The anger really is at the nature of reality. Worse, it is at yourself for leading yourself astray – for not being qualified to handle the freedom you found that you had.

It may be that you are just mad that some people are capable of handling freedom better than you.

It's easy to tell who is capable of handling freedom, and who isn't. Set everyone free and see who handles it best, who makes the best decisions.

If you make bad decisions and ask to be saved from the consequences, the cost is that you lose your freedom.

If you have two dogs, one is well behaved and the and the other one bites people, do you continue to let them both run free?

I can tell you whether you should be allowed to own dogs based on your answer to that question.

Freedom goes to those who can live with the consequences of their own individual freedom. Freedom stays with those who can handle it. Those who can't, won't keep it long.

Which way is the path of the master, and which of the slave?

The Ancient Greeks were free from others, yet they were slaves to custom and opinion. The French today are free to do whatever they want, yet they are under complete dominion of others. Ben Constant calls these opposites Ancient and Modern liberty, Isaiah Berlin calls them Positive and Negative liberty.

The English today have to follow many rules, but are ultimately sovereign, despite what you might think about the 'Anglo-American Special Relationship.' Like the Ancient Greeks, they have Ancient and Negative liberty. Weimar Germany was completely liberated, with few rules, but was beholden entirely to the victorious French Army. Like the modern French, they have Modern and Positive liberty.

There is a difference between a freedom 'to' and a freedom 'from.' One often must trade one to achieve the other, as with the case of the French Revolution, or the inverse with the American Revolution.

What if the only free particle of mass in the universe is one single electron, which travels around the known universe at inconceivable speed to universally simulate all matter at all places and times?

Which type of freedom is more important?

The Magic of Hormones

Until the 1800s, we believed that all phenomena of bodily health revolved around 'the four humours.'

True science of the body is the shot put, which is visualized in the minds eye of the athlete. The object is the definitive placing of this lead ball in that given location – the means to accomplish this is the complete moulding and reorientation of the mind, body and spirit.

It is the chemical composition of the body, the cultivation of raw biological material within a biomechanical corporal mechanism capable of a given and particular task. This task can be to bear a child, run a marathon, fight against cancer, lift a car, or work a desk job for forty years. In all cases, a relative balance of hormones in the body is required.

Yet for the athlete it is not enough to lift heavy things until the chemical composition of the body changes, and the construction of the body acquiesces to a given and universally convergent form – rather it is paired with the accumulation of Will on all levels of one's being, the marshalling of all potential forces and alignment of the mind, body and spirit towards a given objective.

It is the balanced and harmonious structure of one's entire being, the corporal oneness which the ancient Greeks sought, symbolized by the nude athlete, representing an 'altogetherness,' completeness in oneself, not relying on any externalities to fulfil one's unity.

It is not relying on clothes for heat, nor for protection against the elements, nor as a veil to mask one's self-conscious vanity. Nudity is the ultimate show of independent objectivity – for one does not need clothes to mask coldness or shyness.

In this case, for men, testosterone increases both confidence and resilience to cold, marshalling this completeness. Yet, the warlike properties it confers can throw him out of balance and he may become violent and lose self-control. How to create a balanced unity?

Empedocles and Hippocrates developed a theoretical system to manage and understand this balance, which we continued to use until the 19th century. The Greeks and everyone since believed in humours, today, I believe we call them hormones.

This harmonious completeness is a factor of magical substances which, despite our advances in science, have not yet reached a sufficient level to create a truly normative understanding. Thus, we are left at the mercy of a science which follows, yet does not lead the absolute truth. Much like a primitive astronomer, we see the wake of the comet, and observe the wake's properties and from there use it as mere test – formulating KPIs rather than a definitive understanding and means of acquiescence. We can set up the kindling but know not how to spark the fire – though it often does.

The fire, in any case, is something which comes from within.

If the end of science is to manipulate and cultivate this harmony, then we find ourselves at a strange impasse whereby irrationality, a pseudoscience, better attains these ends. It becomes more rational to be irrational than rational. One need not study for many years only to have an incomplete understanding when the mass of mankind be better off with a relatively decent body of knowledge which achieves its ultimate aims as it's end.

The science of the four humours worked – the phlegmatic man was assumed to be affected with an abundance of feminine energy, water, the greater 'yin.' Science only just now sees how estrogen compromises men's immune systems and leads to more phlegm production, yet the Ancient Greeks knew this thousands of years ago. Four liquids in the body had to remain in balance, or negative health effects would emerge. With the correct amount of each, the body would be healthy, and altogether complete in oneself. We also believed that when one had more of one than the others, it effected our moods.

The four humours are Sanguine (blood), yellow bile (piss), black bile (shit), and phlegm (mucus). I believe what the Ancient Greeks who devised this system were really referring to were the hormones of serotonin, testosterone, estrogen and cortisol.

Empedocles, and later Hippocrates conceived of these four humours as each correlating to one of the respective cardinal elements, with Sanguine correlating to air, yellow bile to fire, black bile to earth, and phlegm to water.

The classical thinkers used the bipolarities of the yin and yang in regards to the elemental signs, and superimposed this characteristic phenomenon onto all aspects of reality. We can still do this today to create a working heuristic of the main hormones needed to attain corporal oneness.

Testosterone and serotonin can be conceived of as 'yang,' or masculine, active hormones, while estrogen and cortisol can be seen as 'yin,' or feminine, protective hormones. Everyone needs all four, but to different degrees depending on whether you are a man or a woman, and what your role, age, and circumstances are.

Specifically, they imagined Sanguine (blood/ air) constituting the small white, yang dot, which sat inside Phlegm, (mucus, water) the large black, yin blob, opposite Yellow Bile, (piss/ fire) being the large white, Yang blob, inside which sits Black Bile, (shit/ earth) the small black, yin dot.

Here, I discuss the science of humours, yet I am being completely serious.

Empedocles associated **sanguine** (blood) with air. A person with a lot of sanguine is sociable, outgoing, talkative, responsive, lively and carefree, just like someone with a lot of **serotonin.**

Our serotonin is highest around the turn of the new year, when flowers begin to blossom, and when the summer turns to autumn.

In medieval times, when you were too hyperactive you would go for a bloodletting. A doctor would drain some of your blood and leave you a bit depleted, tired, pleasantly lightheaded and calm. That is because they have drained your sanguine. Traditions across the world have done this for thousands of years – why would they keep doing it if it didn't bring real results?

When you are excited, or exercising, two states in which your serotonin levels increase, your blood pressure also rises. Serotonin deficiency is also linked to low blood pressure. For the Greeks it was far more simple, if you were sad and low in energy, you did not have enough blood, if you were full of energy and vigour you had a surplus of it.

When someone feels romantic feelings, they blush. Blood, sanguine, comes to their cheeks, and they become more outgoing, talkative, responsive and lively. This is because their brain is releasing serotonin in that moment. When someone gets shot, or stabbed, and they lose a lot of blood, they become closed off, unsocial, very quiet, unresponsive, and less lively, just like someone with low serotonin.

When a woman has her period, she finds herself releasing an abundance of sanguine, blood, which had been saved up for the two weeks prior. Serotonin was also saved up, that's why she was so irritable. As the sanguine, blood, is released, serotonin is also released, and she craves love, affection and chocolate.

Seratonin and Testosterone, Sanguine and Yellow Bile both represent the masculine, active element. That is because the kidneys turn blood into urine. The higher one's testosterone, the thicker one's blood is, so that if they get stabbed or injured in combat, they are less likely to bleed out.

When one has thick blood, they are also more resilient to cold temperatures. Thus, when one has a lot of testosterone and a lot of sanguine, they are said to be 'hot blooded.' They are the same essence, just in different forms at different stages. For that reason, Empedocles associated both yellow bile and sanguine with the 'white,' or 'yang' elements in the image of the yin and yang.

The image of the nude male athlete thus represents a state of corporal oneness and independence, in which the blood is sufficiently thick to be comfortable among the elements without clothing. He has not only the thickness of sanguine to remain warm, but the vital spark of life associated with sanguine to attain success in sport and warfare. Sanguine thickness is also why female statues are often depicted with some amount of clothing even if the sensitive areas are exposed.

Thus, Empedocles associated Sanguine with the lesser 'yang,' balanced by Yellow Bile, the greater 'Yang.'

On Yellow Bile, Testosterone, Aggression & Fire

Empedocles associated **yellow bile** (piss) with fire. A person with a lot of yellow bile is aggressive, excitable, touchy, impulsive, active and optimistic, just like someone with a lot of **testosterone.**

Our testosterone is highest in the height of summer, the second harvest, and in the early spring.

Piss comes from the phallus, which is also where testosterone comes from. When you have to piss, and have a lot of it, you are restless, touchy and impulsive. A person with a large yellow bile projector is assumed to be more masculine,[15] and have more fire-like characteristics. In the best of cases, he is seen to be more optimistic and aggressive, the worst of cases, touchy and impulsive. Many social ills in America and elsewhere can be explained in this way.

If you have a lot of testosterone, you are more likely to be very horny. In that case you might try and fuck more people, and the more you do, the more likely your piss will start to feel like fire.

When someone gets drunk on something with a high alcohol percentage, they behave more impulsively, with less fear, they are more active, optimistic and often aggressive. They also start pissing much more frequently, breaking the seal, releasing their abundant yellow bile.

Yet when someone drinks often, they become chronically dehydrated and now we understand they also become depleted of testosterone. In the morning after getting drunk, one is hungover and feels lethargic, anxious, and pessimistic, because they are dehydrated, now devoid of yellow bile.

Testosterone also makes someone more likely to smoke or drink alcohol. When one drinks and smokes, the blood is contaminated, and the kidneys filter it out, making the urine more yellow. Thus, high testosterone is often correlated with more yellow, yellow bile.

---

[15] It's not fucking true damn it!!

The effects of testosterone can be a good or a bad thing, depending whether they have an outlet for this or not, and depending whether they have self-control or not. That is why the Greeks, who had very high testosterone, idealized the image of the small penis. In art, a small penis represents command over one's impulses and desires, making them more capable of handling a lot of testosterone. That is why people often say that men, who naturally have more testosterone than women, often 'think with their dick,' the central organ associated with yellow bile.

The association between sanguine and yellow bile goes yet further. It is why, when men retain their seed, which comes from the same place as yellow bile, it prompts a reabsorption of vital masculine energies into the blood, making them in turn, more sanguine. Thus, a balanced harmony can be attained through the practice of sexual retention. Nietzsche discusses this at length.

When men release too much of the testosterone-producing chemicals through masturbation, they tend to become effeminized – their estrogen levels increase to compensate. The same compensation occurs in society as well. When men become effeminized, women must make up for the lack of masculine virtue by becoming more assertive, responsible, ambitious and dominant, and this upsets the natural healthy balance in the social body, much as it does within the physical body.

Thus, Empedocles associated Yellow Bile with the greater 'yang.'

Empedocles associated **black bile** (shit) with earth. Someone with a lot of black bile is moody, anxious, rigid, reserved, sober, unsociable and quiet, just like someone with a lot of **cortisol.**

Our cortisol is highest during April showers, the August heat, and the winter holidays.

When you find someone waiting on the john, they are rigid and reserved. If you try and make conversation with them, you will find they are unsociable and anxious. If you keep trying to make conversation with them, you will soon find they can be quite irritable as well. People with high amounts of cortisol behave the same way.

Tobacco resembles black bile. Tobacco makes one have to shit and decreases cortisol. Coffee also resembles black bile, in the worst of cases. It also makes you release black bile, but in some cases, it helps you to focus long enough to solve the problem which is causing your cortisol levels to rise.

Contractions of the traverse abdominus also lower stress and puts you in a state of relaxation, in which cortisol is decreased. That is why long-distance runners take a deep breath and compress their abdomen to lower their heart rate. It lowers stress, but if the runner has eaten a meal in the past few hours, it makes them have to shit.

That is why stressed out people smoke cigarettes, run, drink coffee and eat processed food. All of these contribute to the release of black bile, and decrease of cortisol.

In Ancient Greece, people with a lot of black bile were seen as being sober. When someone is stressed, their first instinct is actually to stop drinking, and it's why people who drink can do stressful jobs. People who are stressed at work also take longer and more frequent bathroom breaks.

When someone lies, their stress level, their cortisol, increases. If someone lies often, they are constantly full of stress, cortisol, and retail more black bile. That is why when someone is lying, we say they are full of shit.

People with high cortisol see massive drops in their testosterone and an increase in estrogen. That is because people become stressed when under conditions of attack, and thus their body becomes more defensive and passive, like a prey under attack by a larger predator, playing dead to survive. For this reason, Empedocles saw it as antithetical to sanguine, which reflects an abundance of life and vitality rather than it's opposite, a dearth of life and vitality under conditions of survival.

There is a clear protective and purgative element to both cortisol and this bodily function. In the Bible, Jesus says that 'whatsoever defileth man, cometh out in the drought.' Thus, this fundamental 'yin' element, much like phlegm, which relates to an earlier stage in the digestive process, is associated with self-protection, nurturing, cleansing and the maintenance of well-being.

As mentioned, it shares with phlegm the function of digestion. Much as blood and urine constitute the same fundamental essence at different stages, phlegm and black bile entail two different stages of the same function, in this case being digestion, an act which is 'passive and nurturing' rather than 'active and attacking.'

Thus, Empedocles associated black bile with the lesser 'yin,' balanced in harmony with the greater yin, that of phlegm.

On Phlegm, Estrogen, Selflessness & Water

Empedocles associated **phlegm** (mucus) with water. People with a lot of phlegm are selfless, passive, careful, thoughtful, peaceful, controlled and empathetic, just like somebody with a lot of **estrogen.**

Our estrogen is highest in the depts of winter, the turn of spring to summer, and early autumn.

When you have a lot of phlegm, your voice becomes nasal and high-pitched. That is why men with high estrogen have high pitched and nasal voices. Estrogen is necessary for parenting, especially early on, because passivity and empathy are necessary for the fostering and nurturing of the infantile and weak.

When you have a newborn child, your estrogen increases, and your phlegm, your mucus level rises. This makes your voice more high-pitched, so that you can baby-talk to your newborn child easier, and more naturally. It makes your voice less booming and aggressive, so that the baby will feel more safe in your presence.

Since you have more phlegm and your voice pitch raises, it enables you to teach your young child how to speak, since the pitch of your voice is closer to theirs. A man with a deep voice would have a more difficult time teaching a child how to vocalize words and sounds than someone with a voice more similar to the child's.

Yet for a man, if he is not with child and still has high estrogen, his phlegmatic state might come from other problems. A man with low testosterone will often develop a compromised immune system, leading him to get sick more often. When he is sick often, he will produce more phlegm, coughing up and spitting out mucus. His voice, like I said, will also become more high-pitched and nasal. Thus the ancients saw a correlation between phlegm and behaviours we associate with an excess in estrogen.

The solution to high levels of estrogen is to exercise and to be exposed to the cold. When one goes running, they often produce and spit out phlegm. When it is cold, their nose becomes runny to release phlegm. Empedocles saw this, and thus associated the loss of phlegm with an increase in qualities associated with yellow bile, its direct opposite. What was really occurring was an increase in testosterone, to cope with the demands of exercise and low temperature, as testosterone increases muscle recovery and thickens the blood to make it more resilient to cold.

Additionally, phlegm, which is in the throat, is the first stage in the digestive process. When someone eats food, they are nurturing themselves by providing themselves with nutrients. Thus, a healthy balance of phlegm is essential for self-cultivation, in the same way that feminine energies are necessary for the protection and nurturing of life.

That is why Empedocles associated phlegm with the greater 'yin.'

On England

Free-Form Thoughts, handwritten in the Cotswolds, Burgundy, and the French Riviera Summer of 2023.

Quality can be measured or absorbed, its origins completely unpredictable.

Happy, beautiful and uplifting thoughts.

Antisocial has two nearly opposing meanings in England and America – yet I am both.

Council House and Calm. A rude boy, with manners. A posh boy with a [redacted].

This island bears the correct conditions for the cultivation of a race of cruel, savage conquerors.

The body and mind do little in an absence of Spirit.

The [redacted] should have trained manners. Nothing a bit of LSD and a dinner party can't fix.

Swearing creates a bad impression.

The English have a way of making things both funny and serious at the same time. *Via Media.*

The opposite of bad is good, but the opposite of good is strange.

English science seems to indicate that phenomenon here on earth echoes phenomenon of different cosmological levels. *The Planets, op. 32: 4. Jupiter.*

Being thoroughly anti-aesthetic is gnostic and weird.

Ghosts are constancies of Being which follow repetitive habit, a void and particular form calling itself forward and assuming different content.

How funny must it have been to be invaded by the English?

The British Museum alone justifies the empire; In the halls of eternity lie a Toga and a Top hat.

A Tragedy or a Comedy; France or England?

The most noble people are those who understand Terribleness the best.

True brilliance is a kind which dumbs itself down – and makes itself funny.

Handwritten on Muji 64 Page, Semi-Bleached.

England is the best country in the world. Well, France is the best country in the world, but also the worst. England is technically the second best country in the world, but rather than being outright terrible, it is simply odd, '*gauche*,' left-handed, right-hand drive, and supports its excellence with strangeness. It is better to be strange than bad.

England does this by being clever. It bifurcates and stratifies its intelligence and cleverness, giving all to some and none to others. The latter are liberated, the former burdened. France makes the folly of forcing cleverness on all its subjects, whether they can or cannot be clever, whether they want it or not, to be this French sort of 'clever.' For all this (French) cleverness, which the English despise, they (French) miss the point.

The truly clever reject cleverness. True brilliance dumbs itself down – making itself funny.

That is why Englishmen prefer Happiness, while all the rest of the world prefers Meaning. Nietzsche said (of the will to Power), 'One does not will to Happiness, only the Englishman does that.'

'This Happy breed of men, this little world!' – Shakespeare, Richard II

Muji Unbleached, 64 page. Handwritten.

I was chilling on inner tubes in a swimming pool recently with an Englishman who I deeply respect. We had a long talk, he gave me an honest and detailed assessment of the things I was doing right, my virtues, and where my shortcomings lie, where I could improve.

One of the things he told me was, '[redacted], you need to learn some fucking manners.'

I'm just learning manners now – apparently (and this is new to me) it is kind to repay favours when someone does something nice for you.

So in this chapter I return the favour, giving an honest assessment of this country, what it is doing right, its virtues and where its shortcomings lie.

Irony and piss take aside. I love this country, and I want it to succeed.

What has happened to the city of Newcastle? Stop playing so many damn video games. Better yet, get some exercise and stop beating your meat and getting high all the time. Try getting in a fight. Never thought I'd say this, but you soyjacks need to get back in the coal mines. Same goes for Appalachia in America. Northeast of England and West Virginia, you're of the same stock. You have the same faces and same last names, the same scraggly-ass beards and same colour eyes. And for the both of you, relaxation of tension and rigour results in the descent into the most absolute cuckoldry. When it gets cheap enough just to live, and the means of subsistence for bare life are accounted for, that is when higher orientations of life are most thwarted for you people. That is when the product of all of the work done by previous generations is spent, spent on nothingness and empty pleasures. That is the behaviour of men who seek to be slaves.

You are of great and excellent and noble stock, but it seems you are only able to reach towards your highest potential under the conditions of the most extreme duress. I understand now why Darwin's theory applies only to life in England.

When the means for bare life are accounted for, that is normally when life is able to reach for higher ideals than mere survival. Normally, only under extreme stress does life have only to 'survive.'

Yet this condition liberated from life's demands, is somehow most antithetical to the type of life which is indigenous to the Northeast of England. It makes sense then why England is the country with the largest percentage of its citizens abroad – a strange evolutionary fluke has happened, their homeland has become the place most inhospitable to their own existence and development. They somehow find themselves aliens in their own land. Yet I am not a Darwinist, because neither Darwin nor science, reason or even magic, could ever explain Newcastle's sexual or reproductive habits.

In Newcastle, 90 percent of men are nerds, and 10 percent of men are beastly giga-chavs. Meanwhile, 90 percent of women are sluts, and ten percent of women are nerds. That means, that in Newcastle, ten percent of men have sexual access to 90-100 percent of women, whereas 90 percent of men have access to only 10 percent of women. The North used to be the land of hard cunts, Newcastle was a bastion of Homeric vitality that the degenerated south, with its ebbs and flows of arts and philosophy could lean on. Now it's all video game bars and fried food. Shrek movie night, misanthropy, SSRI Inhibitors, weed, porn, Nintendo switch and weakness. Get a hold of yourselves now or forever be a slave. I should not be able to walk into a random boxing gym, and be the hardest man in there and clean the place out. It seems that London is leaning on an unstable rock if the North really has gone South like I fear it has. I think of Shakespeare, Richard II: 'With eager feeding food doth choke the feeder. Consuming means soon preys upon itself."

There was an esoteric eugenicist neoclassical philosopher in France at the turn of the 19th century called Georges-Louis Leclerc, Comte de Buffon whose theories on evolution were far superior to Darwin's. He believed that dogs only evolved to run in packs in order to take down the big cats. Walk around Newcastle, and you will see just that, packs of dogs, who bind together only to stand a chance in a tension-filled, unspoken war against the big cats - those Celtic monsters of great size and strength, who once gave the city its reputation as the land of hard men.

A big cat against a pack of dogs, who do you think will get the pussy?

Newcastle is the easiest city I have ever pulled in.

I never met someone from Manchester I didn't like. In fact, some of the truest Men I have ever met hailed from Manchester. I climbed Ben Nevis with a gang of hard men, 'gangland enforcers' from Oldham, never have I seen greater Olympic vitality and courage in my life. True noble spirit, cultivated from the depths, there manifest, reaching for something higher, for some noble virtue, high above the clouds. A heroic contempt for life, laughing all the way to the top, along icy Tower Ridge, making a mockery of the fake and [redacted] idea of 'mountain safety,' or 'using ropes.' No, the same mercilessness on others as on the self, or as others might have on you. Take the leap, run the risk, accept the possible consequences, and then have fun with it. That is what the meaning of life is. Laugh at life's hardships and weariness's – that is what it means to be a man.

No wishy-washy back and forth nonsense. You either run the risk or you don't. You either grab life by the horns, and ride it, or you never get on in the first place. If you're on, never let go, not till you're dead.

If you are lucky enough to have been born with, or have otherwise been given the vital spark of the free life, do not ever let it be suppressed. Do not ever let the Lazer be lost in the endless expanse of the mirror chamber of self-consciousness, and caring what people think. If you do care what people think, do it ironically, in a way which makes fun of all of life's tragedies and weariness.

Above all, be too in the moment, too unserious for life for there to be any real weakness to grab onto. I once met a personal trainer from Manchester in a bar in Prague. He was in his late 20s, and could have been an A-list Hollywood actor for his good looks and muscular physique, full head of hair, not a wrinkle on his face, in the prime of his life, he could have been Henry Cavill, but better looking and more jacked. But he was drunk, so drunk, talking about how tiny his cock was, and how he got molested as a child, laughing the whole time and being crazy. He didn't know where his friends were and took off his shirt and started smoking cigarettes inside the bar and couldn't stop laughing while fucking with all the patrons. I've met many Mancunians of the same spirit.

This is true invulnerability, true masculinity, and you could never cultivate the same spirit from example, and play-acting. But, it may be worthwhile to use such anecdotes of carelessness and inner freedom as a test of spirit. In this condition, for all of its naughtiness and careless troublemaking, the true expression of masculinity is allowed to take form, without the restrictions or inhibitions that self-consciousness imposes on itself. At least in this state, you know he is being honest and true.

When I imagine the ancient Greek conquering aristocracy, I imagine these men of Manchester. Similar in their high spirit, their contempt for all the seriousness of life. There is story of Hippocleides, an Athenian nobleman in height of Greek age, when masculine vitality was strongest.

The King of a small but powerful Greek state, in present day Corinthia, brought several dozen prospective suitors to his island, comprised of wealthy, well-bred, handsome and athletic aristocrats from around the Greek world, to see who was best qualified to marry his daughter. This king, Cleisthenes, wanted his daughter, Agariste, to marry the best man possible, so he subjected all of these men to athletic challenges, tested them on wit and conversation, et cetera, to determine who possessed the greatest spirit to carry on the fire of vitality to the next generation of his kingdom.

Eventually, it was down to Hippocleides and Megacles, the top two prospective suitors of the entire Greek world. Yet on the last night, at the dinner party, Hippocleides got drunk, and started dancing on the table. Then, he started dancing on his hands, so that his tunic fell upwards, and he flashed his wiener to the entire party. The King, Cleisthenes, offended at Hippocleides' lack of manners, disallowed Hippocleides to marry his daughter, yelling 'Hippocleides! You have just danced your way out of a marriage!" To which Hippocleides responded, "No care for Hippocleides."

Where else could such human spirit possibly be manifest today, but in the sunbedded hooligans of that city in the North of England? Who else would make such a type, such a mindset believable? Where else on earth can one find this careless vital spirit?

The cowboys in America are far too beholden to others for such freedom, they are bound by the demands of sobriety, work and the serious life, which they lament and pretend they chose voluntarily. Those few still free French, the true heirs of the revolution, who roam the streets on dirt bikes, sun tan all day, get in street fights with [redacted] in the evenings, but drain their vital energy by fucking sixes like rabbits and tranquilizing themselves with Hash and rum, they lack the inner force of power and charisma to muster anything serious or meaningful without the support of the military.

Where else then can you find the spirit of the Bronze Age in our time but in Merry old England? In the Council House, the football stadium? These chavs, who must never be made aware of the spirit they inhabit, their divine significance, the justifying role they play for the human drama, this vitality, this well of spirit from which all moral life springs, now devoid across the world, in a drought, is yet here, yet now, and imminent. But the comet must never see its wake.

These people, those who are of this spirit, they don't even take piss when it comes to the hardest hardships of life – rather, they become dramatists just to make it even funnier. They will only give a clue that they are in on the joke themselves with a sly, devilish and wicked grin that they will flash you when least expected. Who can be so vulnerable, but the most invulnerable man?

It's hard to find love in England when this is your competition. For the higher types, it is yet harder, men of power make weak women feel bad so they run to weak men for validation. No missile can shoot down an SR-71. How else can such life exist, how else can such life survive, but by sporadic hit and run bombing? How much of the female population must be set aside and sacrificed to the whims of this conquering aristocracy of spirit, this less than 1% of men, to be ran through, in hopes that this spirit may be born again? How many English ladies must be set aside to serve as fertile soil, lying in anxious wait, at the whims of the big cats? How many ladies of Britain must be relegated to cannon fodder for these titans of spirit?

And what other choice does such life have, than to be a pirate? Save, to land on enemy soil, and let itself be used for parts?

110

Remember that vulnerability is never a strength despite what manipulative women may tell you. Rather, be so strong that being vulnerable doesn't cripple you. Open your heart and laugh at your vulnerabilities, your weaknesses, rub the soft spots with sandpaper.

Or better yet, just live in England.

Best of all, live in Manchester.

The English approach to life is best summed up in the '*Via Media,*' or the 'middle way,' the motto of the Anglican Church. This means to balance two opposing ideas in one happy medium. That is why English Christianity is a mix between Protestantism and Catholicism, and why the King of England is at once, strangely, both supreme warlord of England and the head of the English Christian church.

It is the secret to England's power and enduring influence on the global stage.

The idea of *Via Media,* manifest in the rest of society, is why everything in England is both funny and serious at the same time. For instance, when someone is hit by a train, the notification you get on your phone does not say *'the train will be delayed because there has been an incident on the railway,'* but rather, it says *'the train will be late because someone has been hit by a train.'* How chaotic. Football fanaticism too is at once, both a piss-take and also serious (whether you're aware of it or not).

It is why even the film Dunkirk had a Harry Styles cameo, and why even Mr. Bean finds love. It is how England can both be the most modern nation in the world while still having the longest running government. Is it funny or serious that the 'average time' on earth can be found in the village of Greenwich? Is it a piss-take that every country on earth uses GMT, Greenwich Mean Time, to coordinate international business, finance, shipping and transportation around different time zones?

England, unlike any other nation on earth, is capable of balancing opposing extremes within one national, corporal body. Nowhere else on earth will one find a greater variety in different experiences of life bound in within one land, people, language, or even one family. It is this unique line which it walks, a tightrope bound together between the fog of prehistory and the jutting peaks of space and time yet unexplored. It is a promise of the eventual reconciliation of all internal opposition, subsumed into the vortex of the absolute standard, the universality of form which this Island lays claim to as its own. It is the promise of a moment, some place in time when all reality itself will one day be realized in a moment of supreme and absolute Being.

It is the principle, enshrined in the spirit, the metaphysics which hold everything together, from the bottom to the top, which holds everything unified in one, keeps focus forward and maintains rank and order. It is the bulwark against chaos, against the atavistic forces of darkness which ebb and flow in cyclical rotation through time and space around the universal axis that is the King of England himself.

'Via Media' is a promise. It is a promise that someday, *it's coming home.*

The political institutions of England are upheld by pure magic.

There is no organizing logic, the political institutions are not organized by logic or rational design like they are in France, America and the other serious countries. Actually, the system maintains itself because the people in charge practice supernatural rituals. The system survives because of magic.

All political power emerges from the Monarch. Passports are issued under his or her authority, Parliament convenes with his or her permission. I will later discuss a mock ritual involving the closing of doors on 'the black rod,' as a show of Parliament's independence from the monarch, but the end of the ritual is nonetheless the black rod entering the house of commons, making the whole show redundant. The functional head of state is Prime Minister, but in almost every other serious country with a Prime Minister, basically just France and Russia, the PM is overshadowed by the President, who holds the actual power.

When this is not the case, it is the constitution which holds the real power. When one joins the American military apparatus, one swears allegiance to the constitution, a common body of law from which all political power derives its legitimacy. England doesn't even have a constitution. The Dutch and Norwegians do, so their monarchies are more or less irrelevant. The Magna Carta is often referred to as the English Constitution, but it isn't. It is a wartime treaty between the King and Aristocracy, not a constitution. The King's physical body is the constitution. The Russian constitution is referred to by scholars as a 'living constitution,' because it is being constantly changed and amended based on political need. Only England has a truly living constitution, the King himself.

Case by case you can go through and see England is unique in the world in this respect. Even Saudi Arabia has had the Qur'an as its constitution since 1992. Israel is at least trying to get a constitution ratified, unlike England, who is happily content without one. England, Canada and New Zealand are the only countries on earth beside Israel who don't have a constitution. They all just use King Charles.

Every morning I wake up and brush my teeth on this little rock in the north sea and remember that I am currently under the authority of a King. Yes, it is the King rules me. The one who was given his authority by God. Don't believe in God? Then who gave the King the right to make all this democracy? More so, how can you explain the fact that things generally tend to work, when that is the only thing keeping it all together?

What is this strange half-nether world, this medieval bastion of the old, wearing a corny hat of modernity, an ancient dragon in disguise, this England of representative democracy? This titan of old, maintaining rank by feudal battle flag, how sweet the sound of its trumpets, the rumbling thump of its mounted charge?

God chose the King. The King lets everything else happen. And you're upset that this is how it went? How much better could you possibly expect such a bizarre arrangement to be? Remember, that rather than political authority ultimately being bottom-up, as is the case of virtually all 'modern nations,' that the British arrangement is completely and fundamentally top-down, in a way that other countries are not.

Yet look how much convergent evolution has emerged, on the surface level how much it looks the same as other countries, real countries, with only seemingly superficial quirks to show the difference. Whereas if one digs down along those quirks, the deeper it goes, the more fundamentally different of an existence one finds in the very essence of the system. The deeper you dig, the more you find everything is completely upside-down.

Only in this condition of upside-downness can the old ways of life persist, only in this condition can the alligators, the dinosaurs continue to roam.

Example. There is a mace, a sceptre that sits in the centre of the house of commons. When someone picks it up, the house cannot continue to debate, they have to stop. Why is this, do you know what the sceptre actually signifies? Do you have any idea what the Sceptre has signified in political ritual, since time immemorial? From Ancient Egypt to the Indus River Valley civilization, unto medieval Britain?

The Sceptre, in this case a mace, has represented for thousands of years, an 'axis,' around which civilized political life rotates through cycles. It is simple physics that in any rotating object, there is a rotational axis, a point which revolves, and 'moves, yet remains unmoved.' The King, sat at the seat of his authority, represents this central point, the 'unaffected,' ie, independent object, relative to whom all others are 'affected,' or dependent. If the concept exists in physics, then to the logic of the earliest executors of political governance, the trend must be universal, throughout all things, ie, must take on a META – physical quality. Thus, in the administration of a political unit, whose context, composition and status is in constant flux and rotation, it must confer upon itself a unit which is unmovable to constitute its anchor, it must find its rotational axis and keep it still, otherwise the revolving object will become unstable and collapse. If the Sovereign is thus the executor of the unified will, he must in his best judgement, be constituted of independent objectivity. In other words, he must not be moved, or had will exerted upon him in any case except by his own volition. The freedom of the nation is derived from the freedom of the sovereign. Thus, he must remain at all times the axis, the *rotational axis*, the sole part of the political system which remains still even when all else is moving. The mace inside the house of commons represents his authority.

In ancient China, the Emperor was consecrated with their authority on the principle that they bore 'immutability in the middle,' and thus bore a state of inner equilibrium, akin to the immovability of an axis and was also represented by a sceptre. In the Bhagavadgita, the 'tree of life' which connects the physical reality to the transcendent bears branches, which when stripped off and wielded by an individual, consecrates 'primordial life force and the power of victory,' again in the form of the sceptre. Myths in Greek, Celtic and Nordic traditions all reflect the notion of the king, or sovereign, bearing a branch, sceptre or mace which serves as the unmoved point in the cyclical flow of nature – the point around which the object revolves, yet does not itself revolve.

116

The word *axle* and *axis* are related. Imagine a cart, with two wheels which spin, held together by an *axle.* The axle does not appear to move, yet the wheels are spinning. Relative to the rest of the wheel, it should be the stillest part of the cart. In the Hindu, Nordic and Greek traditions, the image of the wheel is reflected in all aspects of political life. Whether it be *samsara,* the cycle of eternal death and rebirth and becoming, or the Greek 'wheel of generation,' the centrepoint of the wheel, the part which does not move, serves as the independent rotational axis, at which point the king, the sovereign authority sits. Confucious compares the practice of government to being akin to the north star, which remains steady in the sky while all the other stars move and fluctuate.

Who else but one who wields the stable point of the social and political world can attempt to manage or harmonize the various opposing ends and energies which compete within it?

The Sceptre, the mace, sat in the English parliament today, now, signifies precisely this. It is a two-dimensional object representing the rotational axis of the political universe, with both its north and south pole, as the sole point of stillness and constancy within the fluctuations of the political system. The Monarch, as sovereign, wields his power in accordance with this principle. The Monarch cannot enter Parliament out of tradition, but the Sceptre sits there to represent his authority.

Thus to move the Mace, or sceptre, is to disrupt the peace upon which authority can be executed. You think I am lying? Making fancy and make believe? Having a laugh, taking the piss? Why then is it an observable and measurable fact, that when the sceptre is moved, the House of Commons does not continue to debate?

If your objection is that 'they agree upon this rule,' or that it is out of 'tradition,' and that it is not constitutive then I pose you: why have they, when the sceptre has been moved, not just continued to debate? Why did Cromwell dismiss its power in 1653, calling it a 'fool's bauble,' then still have his troops take it to an undisclosed location that only he knew of?

Out of what fear do the parliamentarians cease to negotiate the future of the nation when the 'immovable axis' is in motion? Do they fear that they will tear everything down?

If they do not continue the debate in order to not disrupt 'tradition,' then I ask, what is the purpose which underpins tradition itself?

I pose you, what else about this country is only upheld because of the mutual agreement to follow 'tradition?'

What would actually happen then if they 'popped the bubble,' ended the game of make-believe, and made the assertion that they will no longer play by the rules of 'tradition,' or 'magic?' How long would the Parliament continue to exist, if the German King and Norman Aristocracy also decided not to play along with 'tradition?'

What manner of monsters lurking in the swamp reign in their appetite only out of 'tradition?'

Do you know about the tradition of the Black Rod? At the annual state opening of parliament, a member of the House of Lords knocks on the door with a special black rod to commemorate the ceremony. But before they enter, the door is slammed in their face – to represent the independence of the House of Commons. Why would they have this ritual practice, but to make the ritual assertion of an active act of defiance? Surely the monarch, with their authority could force open the door, with whom all sovereign power ultimately lies. Yet the monarch tolerates this form of disorder, to allow for this form of life to exist, to allow for the fruits of representative democracy to continue, out of the utility of its function to the people. I imagine the crocodile, who keeps his jaws agape, to allow the little hummingbird to pick away the residues of flesh on his teeth. A willing symbiotic relationship, in which both parties restrain themselves and tolerate the other to allow for mutual benefit. The parliament makes a sham demonstration of their independence from the monarchy. But again, what sits at the centre of the house of commons, unmoved?

Do you know what the crown represents? I am not talking about the propaganda series. A crown, which sits on the head, represents a Halo.

It is the physical representation of a state of being which is both 'inside the world,' and 'outside and above the world.' Much like the sceptre, which unifies the north and south poles, the transcendent and imminent dimensions, the Crown marks the head of the one who had been endowed with being both *here* and *there*. Across cultures, for thousands of years, in different places and between cultures which never had any communication with one another, the monarch has always borne divine justification. The authority which they wield has always derived itself from an 'above,' no matter the cultural understanding of what that 'above' may constitute.

The Ancient Egyptian Pharaohs wore crowns, which represented the divine flame of *glory* given by the gods to consecrate life force and big conquering energy. In Christian iconography, the halo represents being selected by divine favour.

Another example, smaller. In order to reserve a seat in parliament, you have to set a prayer card on where you want to sit. The caveat to this trick, is that you are actually required to pray. Sitting in a good location in the house of Commons is necessary for the execution of your function if you're in a debate, is it then state sanctioned that you are obligated to pray? To what or Whom? Does that infer that the state recognizes that God exists? But we already know the answer to that question. Do we live in an actual, practical theocracy, in which the parliamentarian praying increases their ability to enact legislation?

And you aim to tell me that this political system isn't upheld by pure magic?

Don't even get me started on how the King is also the head of the Church.

Telling me there is no magic at play, though we see its effect, is like telling me that there is no black hole, because we have never seen one. Until that sham-ass photo was taken, we had no more evidence of the existence of black holes than of magic running the British Parliament, for all we had seen were the definitive, evidential effects of both. If science is your god, am I any less rational? In this case, this much is true: I cannot say that I am right, but you cannot say that I am wrong. And thus, with you nerds, naggers and naysayers, I say we are at an epistemic stalemate!

It's too late to get rid of the Monarchy.

After the French Revolution, the Alsatian nobles, the Germanic horsemen of the East refused to bow before the revolutionary government. They claimed that the military treaties they had signed with the king were now defunct as the king was dead, and they had no allegiance to the new French Republic.

Well and truly, what loyalty might anyone with a British passport have other than their individual relationship with that one person, the monarch, under whose name said passport is issued, under whose name their birth certificate is written? Without a monarch, under whose sovereignty all are subject, a reckoning would necessarily occur – begging the obvious question of who is English.

It's very obvious who is Czech or Chinese. Less so with the English.

What does it mean to be English? To have an English passport? If so, that is purely a factor of being under a common monarch. To have been born in England? What about the immigrant born on English soil, who insists he isn't English? What about the immigrant born abroad, who insists he is, or the English woman born in Spain, would she not be?

The Anglo-Saxons of England are an ethnic group yes, as are the Normans, Welsh, Scots, Britons and Celts, and those of Roman ancestry. The English are a people of both miscegenation and individuation – this is because of England's unique sexual habits. The reliance upon alcoholic excesses in mating ritual for centuries has led to a profound honesty in the selection of mates – women almost always go for the best man, by objective standard, that they are able to, and through drinking they become unable to lie to themselves and exercise self-deception on the matter of who they want to procreate with. Men of Britain generally mate for subjective reasons, be it increase of rank, given quirks or physical pleasure. This ensures the maintenance of a 'universal standard,' to which all are subjected.

Looking to other cultures will only solidify this. More than two billion people globally see England as the absolute standard of excellence, and test their own merits and qualities subjectively against it. If truth is a corollary of force, then England is the most excellent and splendid land of the universe. Maybe all of this drama, these dances of the spirit, all of these national tribulations are mere intimations, imaginary apparitions to satisfy the imaginations of what goes on in the land where all things are perfect? Our lives are all mere lore to satisfy the epistemic demands of a universal standard, puppets called forth into existence. Or maybe, those things which we do are those things which sustain it. From where does the correlation between the exercising of our lives and the maintenance of this standard emerge?

The universal standard in English sexual practice thus confers an objective metric at the expense of non-discrimination. Thus, to classify a man as 'English,' as in he looks or sounds like he is from England is simply to say he is 'the best available,' in the way that colloquially, to say that someone is 'Greek,' ie, akin to the Classical Greeks is to say, 'the greatest and most terrible.' The Russians do this literally, with the term '*Saxon*,' as in 'Anglo-Saxon,' while Nietzsche means this when he says that Plato was 'un-Greek.' The national demarcation thus becomes a category above and beyond itself.

The question of who is English would fall on racial, physical or cultural lines. People move around too frequently in England for any true loyalty to emerge to any given locality. People who would die for their football clubs are too stupid to organize any meaningful form of political action. The peasantry in any case can still escape to Spain, the Aristocracy can still escape to France.

Even between the aristocracy and commons, in the question of who is *really* English, loyalties among the non-titular gentry to the aristocracy, and aristocratic loyalties to the commons would muddy the waters of who is who, and when one reaches into the deep repositories of Canada, South Africa, America and Australia, as they surely would, the former would increasingly prevail over the latter in whatever claims they would seek to make.

That is because the only people of European descent in these countries who are aware of their lineage are those whose lineages are recorded – and only people of noble lineage recorded their ancestries. I will explain. The ancestors of English commoners in America do not know they are descended from English commoners, they thus consider themselves only American. In a domestic English conflict, he wouldn't give two shits about who wins in England. Meanwhile, a Canadian who calls himself 'Norwegian' is only aware of this fact because his ancestors invested in family trees to establish locality and heritage. The only reason why they did this was because his family were barons[16]. Thus, this hypothetical Canadian would have a self-conscious loyalty to the Norwegian Aristocracy, while the hypothetical American would not have any loyalty to the English commonfolk.

American and Canadian civic nationalism have never imposed any form of ethnic, inherited or blood-based identity on their subjects – an Englishman might be surprised to find how many white Americans identify primarily with their distant European ancestry. Only a wealthy European of the landed gentry could afford to buy a large enough amount of land in the colonies to have ten children, all of whom who also had ten children, and so on. They now constitute maybe a quarter of white Americans, these descendants from the European gentry and aristocracy, a substantial number, while the rest, descended from the peasantry, do not have the same associations with their ancestral homeland. Considering that the bulk of the American military/ political caste is composed of old Scots-Norman and Anglo-Germanic families of distinguished rank, the British Aristocracy is protected by an 'ethnic tripwire' of sorts.

Military regiments of the British Army are also fiercely independent, and share little to no common tradition to each other aside from a common allegiance to the British Monarch. In the absence of a monarch there is no

---

[16] The Norwegian of noble ancestry who emigrated to America did so because he contested the inheritance rights of his older brother, so the family would compromise by setting him up with land abroad, a very common practice. The deportation of 'criminals' to America was largely a myth and very rare practice, none of the ancestors of these people would still be ethnically self-conscious as Norwegian.

reason why a given regiment in the British Army would have to be fighting on the same side as any other.

The point is, the present arrangement isn't so bad and could be a lot worse than it is. It is better, rather that it is imperative that the monarch, who serves as the immovable axis around which all things revolve and are bound, stays precisely where he is. Those who call for the end of the monarchy fail to see what lies in wait.

All this pomp and circumstance is the wake.

The King is the comet.

On Princess Diana

By idolizing Princess Diana, you are condoning infidelity. Cheating on your husband with ten random men does not make you a boss bitch. It makes you an evil witch. I find it very odd that people will cry about being cheated on, and say that infidelity is horrible, then turn around and say that Princess Diana was a wonderful woman. Pick one or the other – you can't have both.

Charles should not have cheated back, I agree. He should have just divorced her, and left her with nothing but her family's money and a ruined reputation. Instead, he gave in to lust and envy and had an affair of his own. To his credit however, he did marry the other woman and did not sleep around with 10 random women – so at least he did not stoop to Diana's level. Still, in the eyes of the public and the law, they both cheated on each other. Yes, he was still in love with Camilla, but Diana cheated first. A bit of restraint and forethought would have gone a long way. He would have set the proper example for the nation that it is not tolerable to engage in infidelity. Rather, he made a mistake and set a poor example.

The Netflix propaganda series 'The Crown' is an example of what is called 'Whig History.' It presents the old institution of the monarchy as something bad and evil, and the outsider who seeks to disrupt it and tear it down as something good, under the name of personal freedom, self-expression, and science or some shit. In this show, it shows that she gets proposed to by the future King of England and her first response is rally her girlfriends and go clubbing. Red flags for days. Consider that this is propaganda in her favour – how much worse must the situation have been in real life?

I never had any strong opinions on the royals, but after learning what Diana did to Charles, I now sympathize with him and support him completely. It's a good thing he never really opened his heart to her, he did the wise thing, considering what she ended up doing to him. Thank God he ended up with Camilla. She seems like a lovely woman.

England is weird in a lot of ways. That is how they sustain their excellence. But this is not some weird quirk – no, this is a sign of a sickness which cuts to the heart of society. It is a return of the atavistic forces of darkness that had once been buried – now reanimated. The shepherds of society have let the people go astray, they have failed to fulfil their duty and set a proper example for the people to follow. The aristocracy from which Diana came was entrusted to guide the people. I don't know what is worse, that such a specimen, of the highest and most noble birth would fall to such a debased and wicked state, or that the people would find themselves so lost to see her as some kind of ideal, some kind of aspiration. The cult of Diana which continues to this day is something that must be called into question. There must be a national dialogue as to whether it is acceptable to cheat on one's spouse, and whether we should look up to people who commit adultery. England has already done this, had this conversation for others.

If she was unhappy and did not want to be in that arrangement she should have gotten a divorce. She had pictures of King Charles on her wall as a teenager, she was enamoured with him. She got to marry the future King of England, then threw it away because she was [redacted] and jealous.

It is not your partner's responsibility to maintain your mental health. It is your responsibility, and yours alone. A partner cannot help you no matter how hard they try if you do not help yourself. If you cannot do this by yourself, it is your responsibility to seek professional help. Princess Margaret sought professional help for her mental health, Princess Diana was free to do the same. Rather, she thought it more appropriate to have several affairs and humiliate her husband on the world stage.

What exactly was she suffering from, boredom and unhappiness? The fact that she couldn't go out clubbing as much as she used to? If that is really a valid justification for cheating, then no man should ever get with a woman who goes clubbing now. Yet I would not take this stance.

If you still fail to see my point imagine if Adele, or some beloved singer's partner cheated on her with ten random women. Then imagine that her boyfriend or husband went on national TV and slandered her, saying how she drove him to insanity, offered him no emotional support in his needy

126

condition, then he badmouthed her family in front of everybody, saying that they were all super toxic and judgemental, and that the only way he was able to cope was through self-harm and cheating on her with several random women. Then, imagine if all of England took his side. How fucked up would that be? That is precisely what happened in the case of Princess Diana and Prince Charles. Just imagine the situation if gender roles were reversed, and you will see my point.

Is it perhaps because Charles might be considered somewhat ugly, while Diana is quite beautiful? I don't know who needs to hear this, but just because someone is beautiful on the outside doesn't necessarily mean that they are also good on the inside. An aesthetic does not justify an existence. Just because she was beautiful doesn't mean she had the right to do that to Charles.

The idea that she was some kind of commoner or 'people's princess' is nonsensical. She was from one of the poshest aristocratic families in England. Her brother was an Earl. She met the king at one of her family's events. What kind of commoner casually has the future King of England over at a family event? She was as posh as they come, and had nothing but contempt for the lowly commoner who idolized her. Even if she was a commoner, in what universe is it okay to cheat on your spouse, even if they are wealthier and more powerful than you? If the power disparity made it acceptable, then no prince in his right mind should ever get with a commoner – if that's what you want. In reality, she had absolutely nothing in common with 99% of the English public, except for her infidelity and poor fashion taste.

In Kensington Gardens there is a sign commemorating Princess Diana. It says that she used to look at the gardens and sometimes would speak to the gardeners. Of course she would look at the gardens, she was living there rent-free, and of course she would speak to the gardeners, she was probably trying to [redacted].

If a woman looks up to Princess Diana, it just means one thing: that she thinks it's acceptable to cheat on her spouse or partner. Princess Diana being seen as a positive figure inherently validates infidelity. Actually, if she is some kind of role model it makes infidelity something to aspire to. Thus, when one condones the actions of Princess Diana, one is condoning infidelity. It is unwise to look up to this woman as an ideal, unless you think cheating is a good thing.

God punished Diana's infidelity by cursing English women with a generation of [redacted]. For Charles's part, giving in to his own temptations, God cursed English men to fall victim to cuckoldry.

Next time you're on a date with a chick ask her what her thoughts are on Princess Diana. If she says some shit like 'she's a girl boss' or 'she's so inspiring,' split the bill and ghost her.

Let me ask you - how much public disorder in Britain do you think is willingly tolerated?

What the road man represents is an organic and primeval form of life. Observe them, on the high streets of Birmingham, Manchester, Watford and all places in between – look to how they act, dress and behave. See how they are abandoned to a state of pure subjectivity, bound in with the imminent present.

Look at their clothes, their track-pants. Save for the Nike *swoosh*, this garment is identical to the medieval *hose* of their ancestors – how it hangs, how the material is cut. The form it assumes on the body, its functional use. It is, for all intents and purposes, the same piece of clothing that has been worn in Britain for centuries, millennia perhaps. They roam the streets on foot, congregate, drink, fight and make merry, indistinguishable to the behaviour of their ancestors. Without being aware of it in the slightest, they remain in a state of nature which has remained unbothered, undisturbed, unchanged, for thousands upon thousands of years. They exist in an unbroken existential state of being that reaches back, deep into the fog of prehistory, before we can remember.

This summer I saw a gang fight in North London, and one of the guys had a Louis Vuitton scarf rolled into a burgher's turban. I am certain he did not study medieval fashion, but rather found a categorically effective way of employing this piece of clothing in a way that was cool, tactical, and effective. He took this piece of clothing and asked himself, what is the best way, the best function I can use this to suit the needs of my imminent reality? Thus, he rediscovered ancient fashion, in an active, lived and dynamic way.

Ridley Scott uses such artistry. He correctly depicted Jean de Carrouge, a medieval knight as wearing a mullet and goatee, Theo Von style. It seems postmodern and contemporary, but the mullet was worn by Celtic warriors for thousands of years – it was the most effective use of hair on the head for people of that hair type, doing that sort of warfare. The long

129

hair in the back provides padding for the back of the head, and keeps the sun off the neck. The short hair on the front and sides allows the wearer to see unimpeded. Why would a clever and creative French knight not have figured that was simply the best and most effective style to wear his hair?

I do not believe then that this road man in North London then was making a postmodern fashion statement – no, rather, I see that he was living in the subjective and imminent state that postmodernism seeks to rediscover.

The uptick in knife crime then, represents merely a return to the historical norm, a reversion to the natural state of the indigenous population of this island. In neither the case of knife crime nor their fashion sensibilities, are they motivated by a political agenda, nor by some particular acquired taste, but by pure instinct, survival and need, in the same way as their ancestors were.

 They are allowed to remain in this state of pure instinct despite the problems it causes because the managers of this land see that the benefits outweigh the cost. In America and elsewhere, powerful sublimating impulses scrape away this natural state of man from the middle classes – men of still natural nature are relegated to the Ghetto, where they are monetized, raped and capitalized upon by private prisons, drug cartels and fashion brands. Not so in merry old England, where such life lives freely.

Do you think the powers that run this country couldn't stop the road man, or the hooligan from causing public disorder? No, the powers that be in this land see the value, and the virtue in enabling the continued existence of this substratum of society, this petri dish, this primordial swamp of impulse and instinct. They pay great cost for this, this segment creates much social chaos, and the middle and upper classes are preyed upon like the Eloi of H.G. Wells' Time Machine. The rest of society otherwise adopts the approach of the scientist, maintaining objectivity, and go to great lengths not to disturb the subject, this beautiful and primeval form of life. In this state of *samsara,* these folk of imminent transcendence, this privileged stratum is free from the existential stresses which plague the self-conscious castes, living simply and beautifully rather than reaching for

130

something beyond the here and now. How precious this is, this priceless presence in the moment which is maintained only by great care and cost?

How akin they are then to *fauna,* like the fox who roams the London streets – allowed to continue in their natural ways, at most checked and managed?

I ask you, if you returned to this world of unselfconsciousness, fed yourself to this primordial swamp and went native, what place in the natural hierarchy would you assume?

I was in Wiccam – playing football with my best mate in a green between two council estate complexes. There were empty fosters cans and roaches everywhere, trash, you know the sort of place. Some chav youths were running around, but apparently one was in trouble with his father, whose yard sat on the edge of the green. The father opened the gate from the back garden to the green and yelled at the boy. I can only describe what happened next as a close protection operation.

This Chav, and his family executed a perfect tactical manoeuvre. There was a brilliance to it, the kind that is only discovered under a state of rigorous training, or extreme duress. This big man in a vest, covered in tattoos opened the gate, and his dog ran straight out, and knew exactly what to do. It sprinted all the way around the perimeter of the green, all the way around to where we were sat, where he sniffed us out and investigated us quickly but thoroughly. After seeing I suppose that we had no intention to provoke any kind of problem, he ran on, to investigate the other people around before running back to the heel of his master. His wife, during this time, went out to retrieve her son, under the careful watch of the father, who stood at the ready a few paces from his gate. Once his wife carried his son back through the gate, he had one more look around before retreating behind his fence. I remember being awfully impressed with the perfect coordination and tactical excellence I saw. He might have been ex-military, but I doubt it somehow. I think this type of life cultivates natural brilliance.

Perhaps I don't paint the picture well enough for you to see what I saw. There is a certain look in the eye among types who live in the state of
131

nature, the state of danger, of contest and challenge, it is an immersion in the imminent moment, the subjective state, being in touch with the true nature of reality. There is a depth to the eyes, which stares through you, not at you. It does not see you as relatable being, but as an animal, a potential threat. I am not my sense of humour, nor my master's degree, nor my family nor the quirks or peculiarities which people remember about me. I am a 6'4, 15 stone kickboxer with a mullet, and I'm walking towards you.

This type of life is excellent for social and mental health. They are free from the anxious neuroticism which plagues us all, they don't worry themselves with pointless questions like 'the meaning of life.' They are friends with other friends out of a mutual need to band together for survival. Need supplants conditionality, giving it strength and making it look unconditional. When bad things happen, they don't superimpose existential questions onto it, they make do. They are attracted to a given mate for the real reasons, instinctual reasons, that are in the blood. They are free from pragmatic and practical concerns surrounding reproduction and marriage which sterilize us. In an entirely subconscious way, they are free to exercise the highest form of eugenics.

Inversely, if they get broken up with, they are most concerned with the loss of honour, the loss of a given reproductive prospect, and the possibility of the knowledge of their weaknesses being used against them. They are concerned with material metrics which have real affects, here and now, in the real world. They do not superimpose existential questions of personal worth onto the equation.

The end of all this, of course, is to *become.* From this primordial swamp of spirit crawls alligators, small as may be in England, still with the powerful bite. They are in any case, the straight line from the original alligator. They are the pure alligators.

What then of the alligator with a laser mounted on its forehead?

I have no doubt that many of the great self-made men of the Victorian era, who discovered the ultimate truths of reality, who actualized the totality of their inborn potential, all those men of the romantic era who climbed every social ladder and achieved every height of greatness and wonder that had been laid out before them, I have no doubt that this way of life was the path they chose at the end of all their struggles. They realized that the real dream, the real truth, was right in front of them all along. They climbed the mountain, and looking down, realized that true reality was 'down there,' not 'up here,' where there is only rocks and death.

I know because I see their legacy. I see such men in Watford, tall, well-bred and of noble phenotype, physiognomy and phrenology, wearing adidas trackies with their 6 chav kids. If you want I can write a book on Eugenics. They look around, scanning for threats, free from the anxious self-consciousness which pulls those privileged people from the imminent. Knowing, in their subconscious, in their spirit, that this life is chosen, not imposed, chosen, for the virtue it cultivates. With all of its risks and challenges, embrace of danger and the possibility of great consequence and tragedy, but knowing that the virtue outweighs it all as they continually roll the dice in the divine game of chance.

England has thus won a game of chicken, against all other serious countries on the planet. A game of chicken to see who can cultivate and maintain the most intense opposites within one unified political body, with any semblance of political order. France comes close, but finds itself on the brink of collapse. America technically exceeds, though only just barely, but has to incarcerate more than 5 million people, enact totalitarian zoning laws and maintain a fervent police state, and still finds itself on the brink of collapse. This federation can hardly be described as a unified polity. Only England is still running strong – and hardly breaks a sweat.

England today balances opposing ends of the possible human experience more intensely than any other society on earth, perhaps any other in human history. Between two people who might sit beside each other on the tube, one cannot find anywhere else on earth a more definitive expression of the imminent juxtaposed against the transcendent, balanced in harmony on opposing ends of what human beings can consciously experience. England is full of people who believe in science, people who believe in magic, and people who believe in all things in between.

I attribute this cultivated state to either the Anglican Church's principle of the *'Via Media,'* or the fact that Prince Phillip was a Libra. Otherwise, it defies logic and clearly must be a product of magic.

The Ancient Greeks were also stratified – Spartans thought and Athenians fought. However, they never managed political unity until after the collapse of their classical peaks, and when they did, it was under totalitarian rule of outsiders. By then, the great opposing peaks of spirit that had been upheld had come down into mediocrity. They, for all of their greatness, could not manage what the English today take for granted, the unification of these opposing tendencies in one land, language and political body.

It is the greatest piss-take of any human society in history.

English Football and Pub culture was invented by British Aristocrats who wanted to make Victorian England more like classical Greece. The English synthesized the Greek *Apollonian* and *Dionysian* ideas through the concept of the *Via Media,* or 'middle way,' and thus balance the two in harmony until this day.

In the early-mid 19th century, trade routes opened up with the Ottoman Empire, and British aristocrats could, for the first time, travel to Greece, this object of fixation, made relevant by the outburst of neoclassicism in Oxford and Cambridge, as our level of understanding of science, arts and worldly phenomenon came to finally match that of the Classical Greeks. We began delving into the works of Plato, Socrates, Aristotle and Homer and marvelled at their brilliance.

These Englishmen with their new autistic fascination could now go to Greece, explore, and launch expeditions. With teams of hundreds and nearly unlimited budgets from private fortunes and commissions from the British Museum and the ancient universities, they began unearthing treasures and artifacts which uncovered the secrets of the ancient Greek way of life. What they discovered about ancient Greek society was that public life revolved around two main activities: *gymnasium* and *symposium;* or public sport and social drinking.

The Neoclassicists believed that in ancient Greece, human life reached the peak of its potential, with contributions to science, math, art, warfare being unmatched for all history. They believed that public sport and games stimulated the body, while social drinking and conversation stimulated the mind, and that these were the secrets to Classical Greece's vitality and health. These aristocrats returned to Britain with the aim to cultivate a *gymnasium* and *symposium* in their own country, to cultivate similar vitality, which they hoped would in turn lead to Britain being unmatched in science, math, art and warfare.

As they returned, and supported the rekindling of the classical spirit in England, they supported the emergence of thousands of public houses, or 'pubs,' and supported the opening of football clubs in the latter half of the

19th century. They aimed to cultivate both the public spiritedness and physical health of the Greeks through public sporting games, and to change the way the English drank, centring it around public discourse, social connection and the intermingling of people of different disciplines, classes and opinions on various subjects. The Greeks believed that through *symposium,* intoxicated conversation and gathering, they were able to cultivate the *Dionysian* element, relating to Dionysus, the deity of intoxication, and brought several positive virtues to society.

While the Romans were the first to open any sorts of public drinking houses in Britain, in the form of taverns, these differed from the modern pub in that taverns had the primary purpose of being accommodation for postmen and travellers. There was generally one per village. Later, individual families who brewed their own beer would sell surplus drink to patrons creating an early British drinking culture. Later, families ran gin sills, notably during the 'gin craze,' which created a drinking culture that was immensely self-destructive and instead contributed to a worsening of public health. The emergence of pubs in the 19th century radically changed the way the English drank, with a focus emerging on the social aspects of drinking and its life-giving qualities, to cultivate rather than drain social health. During the neoclassical period, they believe that public drinking was essential to maintaining harmony and good social lives at all levels of society, to combat the malaise of the atomized world of the industrial revolution, bringing people together, thus improving mental health.

During the *belle epoque* in France, the emergence of Brasseries followed in this trend, and Russian travellers to Britain were impressed at the public drinking culture of Britan, who returned to open vodka parlours and bars in their own country. The Romantic period, emerging alongside this rebirth of Neoclassicism was in large part fuelled by the life-giving qualities of public drinking, and in Germany, indigenous traditions of the *Hofbräuhaus* took on an increased and expanded role in society, especially in fostering social and political organization.

While football, or games similar to it have been played in the British isles for thousands of years, large and organized football clubs emerged only in the late 19th century. This created an atmosphere in which regional associations and regional rivalries could be expressed publicly in sport, with all parties benefiting from both increased association with localities and participation which improved physical health. With competition pushing individuals to engage in sport themselves, the public became stronger, healthier and more physically capable. The Greeks believed that through *gymnasium,* public participation in sporting games, they were able to cultivate the *Apollonian* element, relating to Apollo, the deity of reason, which brought several positive virtues to society.

Elsewhere in Europe, football clubs began to emerge as well, with a new wave emerging around the turn of the 20th century, emulating this trend. In Paris, they cut straight to the heart of what the Neoclassicists were attempting to cultivate – shooting clubs, which served as one of the leading lobbies for war with Germany prior to the first world war. In any case, all of Europe gradually found themselves entering into a new era of arts, sciences and warfare, with the mental and physical health necessary for the titanic undertakings of the early 20th century.

Industrialization had made public health dismal, and the emergence of public sport managed to cultivate a lasting physical vitality among the public. With this fitting physical foundation, the nation found itself able to rise to yet greater heights.

In Britain in particular and across Europe more generally, this increase of vitality increased both the tension and potential across all levels of society, strengthening both the peasant stock, the bourgeoning middle class and the Aristocracy.

The Great War was made all the more intense owing to the intensity of Will, spirit and health that had been intentionally cultivated just years prior. It was a great good, but with every increase in greatness comes a potential increase in terribleness as consequence.

The Neoclassical spirit, reborn in Britain, spread to Germany. The synthesis of these opposing opposites, *Gymnasium* and *Symposium* found their most terrible expression.

The British Aristocracy, perhaps themselves trying to live up to this Greek spirit, sought to fulfil their duty to their people, and were wiped out in great numbers in the first world war. Later, in the second war, they rose

137

to the occasion once again, serving as the tip of the spear to defeat fascism. The second time around, the German Aristocracy was not there to lead their people – others had taken their place.

Schiller describes that all great historic world events happen twice, once as a comedy, and once, as a tragedy.

Why do I feel this anxious coldness, this tension and distance, this
melancholy, this latent anger? The pot stirred, the defence of evil uttered,
the memory of a world passed, a darkness once rejected, now revived
once again, justified. Spoken into existence.

[redacted] is the political ideology which attempts to impose the rigours
and demands of mountain climbing onto general society.

Ich will Kobolde um mich haben.[17]

In the moment of absolute contest all relativities are swept aside, the
world is transformed into absolute forms.

No longer becoming, but forming a definitive and unified vision of truth.
Being assumes itself.

Under what conditions can beauty preserve itself under conditions of
hardship?

Quickly fading, so that it may return in its exemplary state later, like the
cherry blossom? Becoming poisonous, or in some way terrible, changing
colours to indicate that death is near?

Being proud to combat insecurities is like taking sleeping pills to combat
insomnia – immediate relief at the expense of being more insecure later.

To not lose you must either not play, or win.

---

[17] 'I want Goblins around me,' Thus Spoke Zarathustra

The music pulls us from the pain. But the pain is where the true beauty lies.

Those who are not dancing simply cannot hear the music[18]

Man is animal, yes, but within man is the intimation of something beyond the body. The animal is the vessel, man is separate and divine. I am more than mere political animal.

High and above, outside this world, *Gipfel zum Gipfel,* unimpeded with perfect clarity. *Die Luft dunn und rein,* equanimity to life and death which justifies the former, *die Gefahr nahe.* Master of men, *diese Wolke, die ich unter mir sehe.[19]*

Written on Muji 64 Page, Semi-Bleached

---

[18] Nietzsche, paraphrasing, idk where from
[19] *Peak to Peak...The Air thin and clear... the Danger near... these Clouds, that I see under me.* From Thus Spoke Zarathustra

Without an aristocracy nations are easily annexed by atavistic forces of darkness.

Germany's aristocracy was destroyed at the end of the Great War, and society was left without a spiritual or military vanguard against the coming tide. The National Socialists and the Schutzstaffel quickly assumed the role and position of the Knights of old, reanimating a recently deceased corpse – still clad in its iron armour with fighting sword in hand.

The blood of millions of Germans, spilt onto its soil, seeping into the earth, was enough to awaken the old gods, for centuries at rest, deep underground, awoken again in the consciousnesses of the people. Once put to rest by Teutonic Knights on brutal crusade, the temples and walls built atop their resting sites crumbled under the tide of time.

At the end of the first world war, the German Emperor, Kaiser Wilhelm II and all of the German princes abdicated, abolishing the monarchy and aristocracy. The German Empire was replaced by the Weimar Republic, and Germany became a modern democracy. This new republic faced many problems, including hyperinflation that made it nearly impossible to buy bread on several occasions, widespread corruption, social malaise and political extremism, with various power struggles and coup attempts. Even when people were starving, France would threaten to reinvade when Germany was late on its reparations payments.

Almost worse than these ills was the people's sense of being lost. Mass society had lost their meaning, everybody's understanding of who they were in the world was suddenly overturned. Everyone suddenly had no idea of their purpose or place in the world. The former nobles found themselves commoners, the most debased criminals became opportunists, and found their means. The way out for most was hedonism, the pursuit of pleasure for its own sake.

New drugs being invented, such as Pervitin, a mix of cocaine and amphetamines, and barbiturates became incredibly popular as well. Books can be written on the effects of alcohol on the era. Ways of coping with the residual horrors of war and the existential crisis which followed manifested in the arts as well. *Entartete Kunst,*[20] or 'Degenerate Art,' became extremely popular, including dadaism, cubism, Bauhaus, surrealism, and neo-objectivity. All of these deconstructivist movements indicated one constant tendency – a loss of transcendental orientation.

The feeling which precipitated all of these movements was that a string tying the subject to something above their head had been severed, and it was up to man with his own independent reason and faculties to rediscover their own ideals, their own new purpose and identity.

In its own way, the development of these artistic tendencies reflected Nietzsche's ideas on the path of the Overman. To become the overman, one must become like a camel, then a lion, then a child. First, man had to bear great weight, akin to a camel. Akin to the great labours of the prewar years. Then man had to fight, like a lion. Akin to the war itself, laying waste to Frenchman after Frenchman. In the struggle, he would destroy the old God, the old values, those things which had been previously believed in, demanded, sanctified. Only then would man become like a child again, with his creativity, his spontaneity and direct access to the truth. But the child would be vulnerable.

In this state of vulnerability, the child is creative, he is receptive. But he is also defenceless – and impressionable.

Have you seen the film bird box? What if there was something you could look at, and if you observed it, you would commit suicide? What about something an entire nation could look at, with their eyes, and be gripped by an inescapable impulse, the profoundest will to death?

A hundred years prior to the ascent of the demagogue, his spiritual forbears, his prophets, had sat in dim study, absorbing and processing visual information, light reflecting off of physical surface, Sanskrit scribbled onto ancient linen, into cornea, and became possessed by an ancient spirit, an ancient set of ideas, locked inside the stone walls of temples for thousands of years. This germ, unleashed, this conceptualization of metaphysics and the nature of reality, would germinate and bear fruit in the ripe soil of Germany, transfusing and

---

[20] They didn't call it that themselves

mixing with the dead germs and ideas, the old spirituality indigenous to the locality. This hybrid idea, this twisted paganism killed tens of millions.

Hitler, for instance, believed himself to be the incarnation of an ancient Indo-European deity, an avatar of the Hindu god Shiva, Lord of Death and Destruction, which he told Mussolini at a dinner party. Mussolini found himself in such a disoriented state hearing this, that he had to excuse himself.

One of the people who stared into this forbidden knowledge, locked away for millennia, was Arthur Schopenhauer. His influence on Nietzsche, who adopted the metaphysics which he interpreted from these ancient Vedic texts, would go on to inform the National Socialist philosophical doctrine that led to Europe's destruction.

Don't give me some cucked liberal nonsense about how Nietzsche was against antisemitism, and how he hated the Germans. He was a German, he was giving his people a critique. He 'loved the Jews,' yes, but only because he thought Germans should be more like them. That is to say, not caring about morality, not caring about being good, only caring about personal advancement, and ruthlessly defeating other groups without mercy. Yes, he hated Germans, but only because Germans were too preoccupied with Christian morality and helping the sick and weak and housebound. That is why he hated Germans, they were too merciful, too left-wing, cared too much about the poor and disenfranchised. That is the real Nietzsche, who loved the despisers of the body, those who exalted weakness, because they made way for the overman, who would easily overcome them. Don't give me some progressive wishy-washy whig history nonsense on the man.

What was it, in the particles of light that entered into the eyes of a man in Germany in the 1830s that would possess him – and lead to Germany's suicide and Europe's destruction a hundred years later?

I'm going to tell you.

In Vedic metaphysics, all potential physical and energetic matter in the universe is a form of Parasakti, one of the forms of Parvati, who is the

143

consort, or wife of Shiva, the god of death and destruction. For this reason, Hinduism maintains that all matter and beings are dying and in a state of decay. The Bhagavad Ghita says 'All Things are Passing in Fire,' generally corresponding to the second law of thermodynamics, 'All Matter is Subject to Entropy.'

Think of a comet. What you are seeing is the wake, caused by something invisible, that follows it and gives it aesthetic perceptibility. Parashiva, is formless, yet is the absolute – and masculine form of reality, while Parasakti constitutes material form, the passing and illusory form, the feminine domain of matter, in which you and I exist. You only see that which follows from the real thing, the real thing, you cannot see.

Schopenhauer takes the Vedic concept of aesthetic, or visible reality and calls it the world of 'representation.' The world which we see, is not the real world. The real world is invisible, all which is perceptible merely follows immediately after it. Masculine and Feminine bipolarity are superimposed onto reality and unreality, truth and illusion, transcendence and imminence.

For Schopenhauer the true reality is comprised of the Will. The Will constitutes the 'things in themselves,' or *'Ding an Sich Selbsts'* if you want to be pretentious. Thus, the world is a symbiance between will, on the one hand, the invisible but real dimension, and representation, the aesthetic, perceptible dimension which follows it.

How does this conception of reality justify genocide? In the Bhagavad Ghita, there is a story about a prince, Arjuna, who has to kill his brothers and friends in a battle. He doesn't want to, he is too attached to them as people, as individuals, with personalities. But Arjuna's charioteer, who is actually Krishna, the god of Goodness and Preservation, reminds him that this material reality is not real. Nothing within it, not his friends, not him, not the body which Krishna inhabits are the real or absolute form of reality. Reality, in this conception, is eternal. The bodies, the physical forms, the people themselves, these individuals, they are only an illusion. The imminent is passing in fire.

Fichte, a Romantic German philosopher of the early 19th century, wrote; *'Individuals are only phantoms like the spectrum, not modifications of the*

144

absolute substance, but merely, imaginary apparitions.' How can one care for individual human lives then, when we are all merely illusions, tetrahedrons bound in flames, our conscious selves caught in an endless cycle of life, death and rebirth which continues for all time? What difference does it make if we die of old age, or in a gas chamber or on the battlefield? When one reaches deep enough into the pit of relativity, the absolute relativity of all things, what manner of monster might the looker pull from the abyss?

Stare into the abyss long enough, and eventually it stares back –
Nietzsche.

This darkness, this relativity was once entrenched in the heart of the European. It was quashed first with the Christianization of the Roman Empire, then later with the crusading Teutonic Knights of Christ who put fire to Heathen, and with the good King Alfred's forced baptism of the Dane Guthrum, who had committed wanton genocide against the Christian Saxon of England. A thousand years of blood and fire were necessary to drive out the darkness and burn the plague.

Yet a dormant and dead seed, intermixed with a still-living relative created a reanimated hybrid, an abomination of Germanic and Indo-European, cultivated under the light of a Hegelian sun of reason; an ancient seed found fertile soil in the metropolitan, modern intellectual heart of an old and rotten Europe. Mass mobilization and the creation of a vortex of industry, capital and movement infested its own veins with the remnants of a synthetic, reanimated ancient disease.

To slay this ancient demon, buried deep in the Earth, and locked away in stone temples for thousands of years, now reanimated, now given the reigns of the world's foremost technological and industrial power, the German Reich, the full weight of the British Empire, and the titanic force of will of two billion souls, across India, China, Russia, Africa, America and Western Europe had to be mustered and marshalled for a great overtaking. Only after the deaths of tens of millions, brutal bombing and intense occupation and complete overwrite of social norms and history could this ancient demon be put to rest again.

But the pushback which necessarily followed the defeat of Fascism was the sowing of its own seeds once again, and Britain finds itself next infected with a similar breed of Vedic-derived mysticism. The counter-cultural movements of the 1960s and the sexual revolution, the worship of the imminent moment, the here and now, and the elevation of hedonism to the highest virtue. The backswing necessitates its own forward movement, still yet to follow, still yet to descend. The transition from Hallelujia to Hare Krishna, the great subversion. I won't stand on a high horse, and pretend that I'm better than you, or that I don't enjoy things, or cut loose once in a while, but John Lenon deserved it. I only stand to make the point that the things which the modern person upholds as the greatest virtue is the point of origin of that which they decry as the ultimate evil.

Embrace cyclicality and relativity with the understanding that it is just that. Unless you can escape the box, the platonic cave, you will forever be doomed to this endless cycle of Samsara. The seeds you sow are the ones which birth your own worst nightmare.

But the British Empire, through the study of the ancient civilizations under its dominion, had unearthed its own greatest enemy, the contest against which would mortally wound it, leading to a slow death, the great beast and leviathan gradually bleeding out through the global systems of finance with birth of nationalism spreading throughout the colonies.

Elie Kedourie describes how the birth of the doctrine of nationalism in Germany at the turn of the 19th century following the Napoleonic conquests would directly influence anticolonial movements in Africa and elsewhere in the 20th century. Chandra Bose, one of the leaders of the Indian independence movement was friends with Hitler. There is a famous story about Chandra Bose walking in unannounced and placing his hands on Hitler's shoulders, to which Hitler said, 'Chandra Bose.' Bose replied, 'How did you know it was me?' and Hitler said, 'Because only you, on earth, would have the audacity to approach me from behind and place your hands on my shoulders.'

Think also of the postwar influence of Germans on the American intelligence apparatus and their influence on decolonialization in Africa. I promise you – take a time machine back to a dusty bar in Nairobi in 1961, before they threw the Brits out, and you will meet a German-American man wearing Raybands and a linen shirt quoting the Bhagavad Ghita.

Have any of you Brits seen any German-Americans in linen shirts and ray bands lately?

On the Aristocracy

Free-Form Thoughts, handwritten in London and Switzerland, Summer of 2023

We were only ever internationals to share in God's light, to support all of God's kingdom, not to pilfer and escape.

Among the people, but not of the people. For them, but not from them.[21]

Silly Scots. I will show you the Norman way.

Pagan self-assertion; Christian self-discipline.

Perceval, Indo-European myth of expulsion and return. Youth grows up solitary, strong, swift footed and ascending. Serves King Arthur by chance encounters. Uncouth behaviour and beauty make him a sensation. Slays Arthur's enemy, becomes knight and realigns with his heritage. Across iterations of myth, never a King himself, only a valiant Knight, and never equal with his wife who is higher status.

Monarchy is clearly the superior system. The only reason you wouldn't want it is because you would be too jealous.

What other test of freedom is there, but to be good when circumstances say you have to be bad?

Perhaps [redacted] is meek and has no choice but to conform to the circumstances placed on him by others.

Maybe Jean de Carrouges died in the crusades because his wife used the horses for work.

---

[21] John 17:14-15.

The Knight must prove himself still a Viking (that's why they keep him around, no?)

England is the Doric kingdom, maintaining it's ways only in cruel and warlike condition.

When He comes He bears a sword.

The time may yet come when the King may call on the old Sussex cavalry, when the lions of old are once again let loose on the streets of [redacted] in a day of reckoning.

Everybody wants 'old money' aesthetic until it's time to do 'old money' shit.

Handwritten on Muji 64 Page, Semi-Bleached

In The Republic, Plato outlines the perfect form of government. It is the rule of an Aristocracy of Philosopher-Kings.

The British Aristocracy is the greatest remnant of a bygone age. It is a genetic time capsule, a treasure trove which preserves old and ancient forms of life – for all those old conquerors of the Island and all their inherited biological traits of both terribleness and greatness. It is a millennia-long breeding project, with its reason for existence split between two competing tasks – for the women it is the production of a biological specimen of the highest order. For the men, it is the orientation of society towards transcendence through the guidance and protection of the people.

Among the English peerage, I have found some of the best people I have ever had the privilege of knowing. Some of the most noble, kind, and generous characters, and yet, some of the most well learned, brilliant, insightful and wise people I have ever known. They are truly a blessing of mankind, and if ever God was to come down and demand for the human race to justify itself, call for us collectively to justify our existence, many of those who would step forward would bear titles.

To be noble is to mean two different things. On the one hand, it relates to character, to be of good morals, generally corelating to the Christian idea of self-discipline. On the other hand, it means to be free, like the noble gas Xenon, which does not interact with other elements, sovereign and uncorrupted by society and its socializing effects, akin to the Pagan principle of self-assertion.

The synthesis of these two opposing and competing ideas serves as the crucible, the ball of immense stress and heat from which higher life emerges. The greater one increases one aspect, the more difficult it is to retain the other. Strong is the man or woman who can balance both to the highest degree and actualize the higher medium.

This type of life is the ultimate manifestation of the *Via Media.*

In order for this life to exist, much less for it to flourish, it requires specific conditions. It must be liberated from the demands of mere subsistence and it must be liberated from the demands of social norms. It requires the preservation of one's inner state of nature.

But today much of the British Aristocracy has fallen victim to a profound corruption. Their destiny beckons them downwards. They have fallen victim to a mistaken belief – that they were born automatically deserving their privilege and honours, without the need to justify their position. They think that all their wealth and status is theirs to begin with, that their specially selected genetic stock comes to them for free, without obligations.

Worse, they think that the purpose of their inherited abilities and privileges, physical, monetary, social or otherwise, is to enjoy life and maximize their pleasure. They mistakenly think that they have a right to the privileges, but are not bound by the duties which accompany them. And so, they enjoy cocaine, copious drinking, promiscuous sex, MDMA and all the frivolities of life with impunity and disregard. They seem to forget that their ancestors were only given their titles, land and wealth for some given and particular purpose, not for its own sake.

In the 1840s, Empires across Europe began to modernize and centralize. As cheap grain began to be imported from colonies in massive quantities, freeholders and peasants could not compete on the market. Thus, they were forced to move en-masse to cities, and live in squalid tenements across Europe to find work and survive. The peasantry was mobilized, and they were forced into the vortex of industry, where atrocious living and working conditions entailed living hell for those who had once tilled the soil.

The Aristocracy across Europe quickly stepped up to protect the peasantry from the predatory new class of industrialists. The term 'Landespatriotismus,' Land-Patriotism emerged, in which both the Aristocracy and the Peasantry were aligned with a common identity, a patriotism towards the land itself. In Germany, Austria and elsewhere, the Aristocracies, entirely on their own volition, lobbied and wielded their ancient powers to slow or halt the alienating process which saw man reduced to cog in machine. Thus, in these places, ancient and primordial forms of life continue to exist until this day, a tradition of country living which maintains its natural order and function. Meanwhile, in many other parts of Europe, the countryside has been swept clean of those who once lived there, as has the rich ethnic culture they may have once had.

Because of this *Landespatriotismus*, which culminated in the Revolutions of 1848, Aristocracts across Europe were able to re-justify their existence. They took the initiative to stand up for their people, to protect them from the merciless captains of industry. They showed that they were unafraid to fulfil their ancient purpose in modern times. They accepted the responsibilities which came with their privilege. For this reason, the Aristocracy in Germany and Austria was given far more power, relevance and authority for the next 70 years, for they had earned their respect once again, that is, until the Great War beckoned the end of Europe's noble and imperial institutions.

Napoleon had sought to destroy the Aristocracies of Europe in his rise to power. But the Aristocracies showed themselves to still be noble.

Who among you would still be noble today?

'The loss in respect in authority... (it) came when industrialists and bankers replaced the warrior nobility.' – BAP

Pleasure is not the end of life. Transcendence is. A child might enjoy chocolate, but would do well to not eat too much of it. John Stuart Mill says that 'if pleasure was the ultimate aim of life, then a pig rolling in the mud would be better off than a slightly irritable Socrates.' Who among you would rather be a pig than a philosopher-king?

Aesthetic and pleasure are just flavours on a spectrum. One must ask, what is the end of this? When one elevates forms and flavours to the highest virtue, they make their reality devoid of essence and content. We can see forms, taste and flavours insofar as they indicate something else – but looking to them as the important aspect in themselves is a deception. Fresh meat tastes good and is free of bacteria. It can also taste bad and be free of bacteria, or taste good and be full of it. Aesthetic can be deceptive. God gave us more than eyes.

How many today cry about the lack of meaning, or point in their lives, and then turn all the more towards those things which obscure the meaning which they seek? They pity themselves over their miserable state of nihilism while still enjoying the vices, pleasures and excesses which keep them bound in this state. As their self-pity then increases, they turn against the higher orders of the spirit which they have forsaken, and cast it down, denigrating it and making mockery of it. They say that it is them who has been forsaken, but who bought the coke?

They make a great display of having chosen their downwards path willingly, as a statement, to make a point. In reality, they lacked the strength or self-discipline to deny those things which engendered their own alienation in the first place. Thus, they champion their own enslavement. The higher spirit which sought to be marshalled upwards dissolves into the wind. Stop watching Rick and Morty.

If you point the bow of a ship to port, where will the ship eventually go? If you kick a ball, and you're looking to the right, where will it go? If a nobleman keep his eyes towards vice and degeneracy, tell me then, where will he go?

An Aristocrat has a title because a King gave him one. A King derives his authority from God. Thus, the King saw noble spirit and capable character akin to the Godly ideal and decided to consecrate that person's bloodline to fulfil a given duty. Therefore, if you don't believe in God I see no reason why you should have any pretension about noble titles. Thus I will invoke a biblical idea.

There is an idea in the Bible that God gives to those who do well with what they have, and takes away from those who don't.[22] If an Aristocrat uses his money on drugs, his title to bang women, his passports to escape taxes, do you think that God, from whom his title is ultimately derived, will let him keep his wealth, power and prestige for long? Or would the

---

[22] Matthew 25

stars align in such a way that he would lose it all, and end up penniless and alone?

In any case, it's too late for most of you now. The best bet is probably to beg God for forgiveness and hope for the best. It's not so bad to be a peasant – if you can get so lucky.

Fifty years ago most aristocrats listed 'sportsperson' as their primary occupation. Participation in Football clubs can be an excellent means to cultivate public spiritedness and a solid physical foundation. The masculine virtue which they bring is a great good for society, it makes life ripe for great endeavours of body and spirit. However, it must be recognized that football club fanaticism is ultimately a piss-take. It was never meant to be that serious. If you don't get that, then you've missed the point.

The Neoclassical thinkers of a hundred-fifty years ago, who started the first English football clubs, chose to make football in particular the sport of choice for the British public because it made for good foot soldiers. It helps with mobility, coordination and organization, while keeping its players quick on their feet. You don't have to be aware of this fact in order to enjoy football, and you can be aware of this fact and still enjoy it. Men in the social circles of Sir John Sloane and others attempted to rekindle a fire in the national spirit which they felt had been burnt out. They had missed the *'Landespatriotismus'* wave, and wanted to compensate by giving the working class atomized masses of England new fidelities to support.

Any person who purports to be noble should be aware of this. The club itself is a means to an end, not an end in itself. If you want to serve your locality, re-enact the sort of public service of your Knightly ancestors, feel like you're part of a team, one among many, and fighting for your local people against the strangers from another town who disrespect you, there's more effective ways than to just be one more cheering fan in a football stadium. You're not actually fulfilling your inherited duty by participating in football hooliganism – even if it feels like you are. You can

154

still support a team, in fact it's a good thing if you do, but don't have some false pretension that you are not obligated to do anything more for your people and locality.

If you're not into football, try playing Polo and doing community service. Soup Kitchens need your time more than merch companies need your pounds. In any case, the responsibility you have is to protect and guide the people. I say play Polo because a man on a horse can do a lot more than a man on foot – if you have the means and know-how to ride one well. It doesn't just make it easier to *guide* a flock on horseback. There is a reason why horsemen since the dawn of time have constituted the aristocracies of Eurasia.

When you understand this, it makes sense why noble people were given land as well as privilege and titles. In each case, they are means to specific ends. They get privilege and land at the cost of responsibility, giving their lineage the right to retain a still-natural nature, a capacity for evil, on the condition that they use it for good.

Those who lose their privilege ought to ask themselves 'why.'

Often they join the atavistic forces of darkness which simmer beneath the surface, or they pretend they never had any responsibilities to begin with. In both cases, they would be better off re-joining the very peasantry that they look down upon, and allow a few generations to pass, and try to cultivate that spark of vital life force which orients upwards. Perhaps then they can re-enter the state of purgatory that is the gentry, in hopes that their bloodline may one day bear a title again.

You look up, because you long to be exalted. I look down, because I am exalted. – Nietzsche.

I say this because many might forget that their ancestors had the best mating opportunities – they skimmed the cream off the top of society for hundreds of years. Their knowledge of breeding dogs and horses was applied to themselves, so as to create a race of noble warriors, capable of great endeavour and the moral character to do it righteously. Yet many aristocrats today make the mistake of choosing airheaded models or

155

actors as brides or husbands, devoid of noble or warlike qualities, enjoying them as objects of aesthetic pleasure. This creates children of decline – morally, spiritually, intellectually and physically inferior to their forebearers. Rather than employing the same selective tactics which strengthened the stock of their ancestors, they just like having a nice piece to fuck on. I would be a hypocrite to say that one shouldn't get with models or actresses, because there is often a correlation between beauty, height and noble characteristics, but only because these are all mutually the product of something else and not the ends in themselves. Good warriors who are selected along generations for noble traits are generally tall and beautiful, but not everyone who is tall and beautiful is necessarily a good warrior or of noble character. A woman can be tall and beautiful and dumb as a rock, and desperately wicked. Again, God gave us more than just eyes.

An ounce of discipline, forethought and restraint would be almost enough to fully right this problem. Thinking perhaps about lineage rather than just having a nice piece of fuck meat in the here and now would do those in power well to preserve their position, if they suddenly found themselves deserving of such a fate. Yes, but more than just some sexual discipline, maybe a bit of self-control and not sniffing so much coke might do the trick. Or would have. Going to church once in your life might help a bit too, rather than the same shitty bar or nightclub you fish in three times a week. Thinking of teleology, outcomes down the line, maybe something a bit further than what you see with your eyes would be best of all.

Save for the excellent work of the House of Lords, and the charitable contributions of the Royal Family and other noble families to various causes, the people in many ways have been robbed and abandoned, with a promise still yet to be fulfilled – the likelihood diminished each time another duke, earl or baron takes flight, like a corrupt bureaucrat, robbing their country and fleeing with a briefcase full of cash.

Perhaps a bit of memory regarding what got them to the place they are in now would be of help, and maybe a bit of gratitude to their king for dubbing them knight and not beheading them, more generally to their nation for putting them up in castles, manors and estates for so long, rather than calling them 'povo,' or 'plebs.' Is it any wonder that the people, those commoners whom they were sworn to protect, also find themselves lost in this way? Is it any wonder why the common folk want to 'eat' the aristocracy? Who could blame the common folk, for the atavistic misanthropy which boils in their veins, which reddens their bloodshot eyes? The Aristocracy look back at their icy gaze with wide eyes and a hundred pound note rolled up in hand, asking, 'who, me?'

Yet I still hope the Aristocracy chooses to right itself. It would be too great a tragedy for the bloodlines of the greatest race of conquerors in the history of mankind to be relegated to history books as has already happened in France and Russia. Unfortunately the enemy is a lot closer to the gates than one might realize, the day of reckoning is much nearer than you might think.

A coat of arms is only an image. Noble is an attribute of character.

The existence must justify the aesthetic.

Maybe if the best among you can right yourselves, make it not 'too little, too late,' then one day the Good King William, a Cancer himself, having weathered the storm and battened the hatches, may let loose the sails of an unapologetic and reanimated England upon the High Seas once more.

Those among the privileged caste who retain their Noble nature have all of my respect.

Those old guard, who were entrusted to watch the seas, what have they come to? They speak their minds then apologize. I say what I mean and wear Kevlar.

On Philosophy - Epilogue
Free Form Thoughts, handwritten in London and the Cotswolds, Summer of 2023

The eternal moment of being, the peaks upon which one sits, the clarity with which one speaks. To go from peak to peak, *one must have long legs; must be Great and Tall.*[23]

Zen is equanimity in a bored state.

Much as one can observe the properties of a single drop of water and deduce all the characteristics of all the waterfalls and oceans of the world, so too can one do with a single human being.

If you ever see paparazzi just start [redacted]

Embrace the good too with equanimity, you can't be perfect. We must fall in order to rise. Ask yourself how the sheikhs justify their wealth and consumption, complete and utter detachment.

Let that be your next challenge, breathe now but do not think yourself absent self-overcoming.

Free modes of thought and absolute being, those who have these are blessed and consecrated. Those who take the risk, dance to the tune of contingency and chance.

A [redacted] is a madman who articulates his madness. Ergot is poison, what of LSD?

---

[23] Thus spoke Zarathustra, Nietzsche

Be not the tree which burns, nor the man engulfed in the fire of his house, but that man who masters the wood to heat his hearth.

Darkness and fire are parts of this life, but who masters who?

Only Saddam Hussein ever felt the full weight of the Anglo-Saxon war machine.

America should just cut its losses and join the commonwealth.

An aesthetic cannot justify one's existence, the existence must justify the aesthetic.

Science doesn't deserve martyrs.

Average yellow press enjoyer.

Cigarettes trade health for aesthetic justification.

Handwritten on Muji 64 Page, Semi-Bleached.

I hate philosophy. Philosophy makes you ugly. We have known this for thousands of years. Read descriptions of Socrates. It contorts your face, turns you into a monster. The self-consciousness necessary for this pursuit induces stress which melts away the naivety, the unification with nature from which beauty springs. In contemplation of the subject as the object, one defiles nature. In response, nature strips away her gifts. In rejecting the aesthetic, and seeking only that which is within, the aesthetic rejects you, and what is within, is all that shall be sought of you.

I hate writing philosophy. I have to tranquilize myself cigarettes and force myself to sit still when I would otherwise be bouncing off the walls with energy. I am a man of Sanguine, of blood. To write philosophy, I must pull myself from my exalted state of imminence and presence and cast my mind from my body. I must observe, but not enter state of Being. I muddy the waters of my soul with thick, heavy boots. I become anxious and self-conscious, aging myself quickly. I become stressed as consequence – and I lose my positive virtues, few as they already are. I transmute the beautiful things inside myself into abstract intimations. Real truth is transformed into mere words, vanities, made digestible and transmittable.

Human beings are natural landscapes of untouched beauty. Pen and paper are excavators, dig teams in search of coal.

Yet this allows a metric of absolute value to be applied to human beings.

'The Will vanishes on contemplation of itself.' – Nietzsche, Birth of Tragedy.

Philosophy begins in the body. Only from a fitting physical foundation can the well spring. One must have abundant Will in order to transmute it to truth. Will emerges insofar as one is in tune with their nature, insofar as their four humours are well-balanced and in harmony.

My ancestors were bred for a thousand years to be savage and domineering warlords in the hills of Scotland. I have thus inherited a body of suitable physical foundation and a mind capable of relativization. Neither my mind nor body were made for philosophy, but they can be used for it. Philosophy begins in the body, under a solid physical and hormonal foundation, and then rises into the mind, transmitted into the consciousness as intuited knowledge. From the peak of the mind, it
160

becomes receptive to interpolations from beyond. The highest form of philosophy is theology.

In order to know what you don't, you must sacrifice what you have. You transmute the inner power within yourself to reach the higher orders of knowing. In doing this un-natural crime against nature, you unlock her secrets. That is why ancient Oracles who foretold the future were always products of incest. Foucault is not wrong then when he says that power and knowledge are one and the same insofar as an increase in one is an increase in the latter. But those he critiqued were still right that one must nonetheless sacrifice one to attain the other.

Many, over my life, have speculated to what goes on in my brain. I will tell you. When I am sat at a desk with a view, say of some mountains, I am possessed by an impulse to go into the mountains. I do not want to stay sat there, and write – I want to go, and take action. I seek to expand myself over space across time, and in doing so, master them both. That is what my impulses command me to do.

For instance, I used to want to be a race car driver, but then I realized that it was just the impulse to master space and time. So I moved to eastern Europe and undertook the discipline of geopolitics.

But when I have some cigarettes, I am content to just go onto the balcony and observe the mountains. That is because a cigarette is a tool of sublimation, and gives a few moments of satiation, a few moments of aesthetic justification, whereby life is lived in experience. Life and will, directed against the self, liberates the body from the demands of spirit. The base the mind rests upon falls, and that accumulated truth falls down, to the hand. Real truth, lived unity, is made profane and sold.

I observe the distance between the self and the mountains I am observing, and gradually, I lose the distance. That distance, the difference between the self and the mountains gradually fades away, and within my body of consciousness, I become unified as one with my external surroundings. I become myself, an object of phenomena, no different to the mountains before me. In this state, my thoughts become liberated from intermediating between the self and the external, and I enter into a state of objectivity.

In this objectivity, I see things that I would not otherwise see. I can study and observe, from a distance, both myself and the relationship between my self as object and the world around. I am at once subject and object. In this state, I am capable of philosophy.

It is not healthy to smoke cigarettes.

If I told you who I was, maybe then you might believe the things I have to say. Maybe you might say 'oh, he actually knows what the fuck he's talking about.' So I won't. I hope that 99% of those who read this emphatically disagree with what I have said. Both in principle, the moral grounds from which I speak, and in the very premises and theories from which I draw these conclusions.

I hope you don't believe what I have to say. I hope the lot of you discount this book completely, it will make you all the easier to [redacted].

Philosophy is a symptom of a sick and dying society. I walk the line between Sparta and Athens – I offer you the antibodies.

Now is the time for Filosofy – with an F.